BIG MAMA SAID:

You Will Understand It Better By & By

CORNELIA S. GARRETT

ARPress
45 Dan Road Suite 5
Canton MA 02021
Hotline: 1(888) 821-0229
Fax: 1(508) 545-7580

Ordering Information:
Quantity sales. Special discounts are available on quantity purchases by corporations, associations, and others. For details, contact the publisher at the address above.

Printed in the United States of America.

ISBN-13:   Softcover   979-8-89389-496-7
                  eBook   979-8-89389-497-4

Library of Congress Control Number: 2024918976

TABLE OF CONTENTS

Dedication Page I

Chapter 1 : In The Beginning..1

Chapter 2 : Train Up A Child..7

Chapter 3 : Have Faith As A Mustard Seed....................21

Chapter 4 : You Got To Live In This World....................24

Chapter 5 : Rock Of Ages Cleft For Me 41

Chapter 6 : There's A Preacher In The House..................46

Chapter 7 : Plant, Water And Watch It Grow..................54

Chapter 8 : Tamara You Got To Deal With It!.................64

Chapter 9 : No Excuses 84

Chapter 10 : Let Not Your Heart Be Troubled 90

Chapter 11 : Life's Raging Storms Require An Anchor! 129

Chapter 12 : Are You A Covenant Keeper? 146

This book is a promise I made to my "**Big Mama**", Cornelia Cousins-Hairston: To remember and write about the lessons she taught me as a child. Reverend Cornelia Cousins-Hairston was a God-fearing, holy servant of God who believed to achieve pure happiness one must faithfully trust God, "**Make him the number one priority and everything else falls in line**." Her guidance and dedication to my spiritual growth helped me form and practice a spirit-filled walk with God as a child. She led and taught by example what it truly means to have natural care and concern for your fellowman. Though I might not have totally understood the lessons and the stories she shared, big mama said, "You will understand it better by and by."

Cover Picture by Cortez T. Wall

DEDICATION PAGE

In memory of my momma: Edna Mae Garrett, whose last request was for me to "Stop stopping and starting my life for everyone else's crises and to live the life God called me to." Thank you for your recognition and release.

To my Aunt Leomia Ross who when I shared my vision told me "Child, write and speak all you want for somebody wants to read and somebody wants to listen."

To my precious "**Big Mama**" Rev. Cornelia Cousins-Hairston, you are forever loved, appreciated and never forgotten.

A special thank you to my cousin, Velma Rodgers, for giving me the lift I needed to complete this book. The question "What are you about?" It made me realize I had planted for years in a garden I had never harvested.

Thanks to Pastor Staples of St. Matthews United Holy Church Bluefield, West Virginia, my Pentecostal mentor. Bishop Clarence E. Moore, Greater Mt. Zion Pentecostal Church Bluefield, West Virginia, my spiritual motivator. Bishop Alfred A. Owens Jr. Greater Mt. Calvary Holy Church in Washington, D.C., my spiritual father. Thank you from the bottom of my heart Pastor Bonnie Hunter for your display of friendship and compassion when I needed spiritual healing. Always my "Spiritual Friend". And thank you Pastor Bernard T. Fuller for the opportunity to experience God's global kingdom building process.

Thanks to my family and friends for their support and encouragement. Special love and thank you to my daughter Harmony for believing in me as I set and kept my eyes on the Lord Jesus Christ following his will for my life. The results of **our** sacrifices have led my family and friends to establish personal relationships with Christ.

My earnest prayer is that young children will develop Godly characteristics that will help them walk by faith and not by sight. I pray this book will touch lives and stir the hearts of all that read it to think and to pursue the gift of eternal life that is waiting for each person that believes Jesus is Lord and Savior.

To God Be the Glory!

We'll Understand It Better By and By

By Charles A. Tindley

We are tossed and driven on the restless sea of time;
Somber skies and howling tempests oft succeed a bright sunshine;
In that land of perfect day, when the mist have rolled away.
We will understand it better by and by.
By and by, when the morning comes,
When the saints of God are gathered home,
We'll tell the story how we've overcome,
For we'll understand it better by and by.

We are often destitute of the things that life demands.
Want of food and want of shelter, thirsty hills and barren lands;
We are trusting in the Lord, and according to God's Word.
We will understand it better by and by.
By and by, when the morning comes,
When the saints of God are gathered home,
We'll tell the story how we've overcome,
For we'll understand it better by and by.

Trials dark on every hand, and we cannot understand
All the ways that God leads us to that blessed and promised land;
But He guides us with His eye, and we'll follow till we die.
For we'll understand it better by and by.
By and by, when the morning comes,
When the saints of God are gathered home,
We'll tell the story how we've overcome,
For we'll understand it better by and by.

Temptations, hidden snares often take us unawares,
And our hearts are made to bleed for a thoughtless word or deed;
And we wonder why the test when we try to do our best,
But we'll understand it better by and by.
By and by, when the morning comes,
When the saints of God are gathered home,
We'll tell the story how we've overcome,
For we'll understand it better by and by.

CHAPTER 1

In The Beginning

John 1:1
In the beginning was the Word and the Word was with God, and the Word was God.

Matthew 7 verse 7 says, "Ask and you shall receive; seek and you will find; knock and it will be opened to you. "High on a hill was an old rugged cross." "Big mama what's a rugged cross?" I asked "Shh! Just listen," she replied. "Ask and you shall receive, seek and you shall find, knock and it will open." I repeated to myself. The man kept talking. "Saints we know that God is our strength and refuge in times of trouble. We can look to the hills from whence cometh our help and know! That our help cometh from the Lord! We must meditate day and night on God's words." "Big mama what does meditate mean?" I asked. "Meditate the word is meditate. It means to think about something and be quiet. And that's just what I need you to do right now." She said. My goodness, I don't know what to think about, but I know I had better not ask her again. Hmm! What should I think about? Ask and you shall receive, seek and you will find, knock and it will open. I wonder what all that means. Who should I ask? Big mama doesn't want to be bothered right now, and I better not seek anything in here cause she told me not to leave my seat. Knock! Oh my God if I start to knock, I know I will get in trouble what should I do? I chuckled to myself. "Shh!" Big mama said again. Maybe I should think about the old rugged cross. I guess I could ask my teacher when I go to school. I had better meditate on it so I don't forget.

"Baby sister, wake up let's go. Church is over." Said big mama smiling down at me. "Sister Collie, this is my great-great-grand baby named after me, the one I've been telling everyone about. You know she's the one." "God bless you little sister and you keep coming back so that God can do great things in your life, you hear me good child. God got something special for you and you can't find out what it is if you don't know him. Have you found him yet?" "Yes mam!" I replied. After big mama had introduced me to everybody in the church. She wanted to introduce me to the pastor. I was tired and hungry, and I wanted to go home but I knew she wouldn't rest until she had her way. "Pastor Blaine this is my great-great grandbaby the one I told you about the one named after me," she explained. "Yes mother." Pastor Blaine said flashing a big smile. "I want you to pray for her, she's special to me and I know she's the one!" Big mama said as she gently pushed me towards him. I'm the one I thought I'm the one for what? They looked at each other and smiled and all the people gathered around me and prayed while the pastor patted oil on my head.

As we walked home, I had a boatload of questions for big mama. "Big mama I was thinking about school and when I get there, I want to learn about the cross on the hill that can give me help." I said. "Baby, you don't learn that in school, that's why you come to church." She replied. "Oh!" I said puzzled. "Well let's go home and eat and I will explain it to yah." She smiled that loving smile, held my hand and hummed a hymn as we walked slowly home.

When we got home. Everyone was glad to see us. My sister, Ladybug, could not wait to ask me what church was like. Everybody else couldn't wait for big mama to declare it was dinnertime. My little brother, who we called "Mr. Knucklehead", started to laugh and joke. He said, "I hope it wasn't one of those Holy Ghost filled services today cause if it was big mama won't stop praying before the dinner gets cold." I tugged on big mama's dress and asked her what Holy Go was. She didn't look to happy and asked me to stop asking questions. She would explain it to me later, "just go and get ready for dinner." I ran upstairs, washed my hands, changed my Sunday clothes and returned to the table. Everyone held hands and big mama prayed. It was the time of day I loved, because everyone was always there. Big mama says that a family that prays together stays together. My brother, Vandy, says if you want to eat you had better be there when dinner is served.

After dinner, my oldest sister, Tyra and my oldest brother Vandy had to clean the kitchen. If it was a nice day like today, big mama and I always sat on the swing on the front porch. I always went to sleep on her lap but today I was determined not to go to sleep. I needed to know about the cross on the hill that gives help.

When we finally got comfortable in the swing, I started to shoot questions at big mama. "Where is the cross on the hill that you can look for to help?" I asked, "What baby?" She replied. "You know in church today that man that was up front said the cross on the hill he could see it and it was going to help he said he knew it would." "Oh, so you did listen a little bit," she replied with a smile. "Well, the man up front is a preacher, Pastor Blaine; he is the one who teaches us what we need to know about God and Jesus. The cross is how Jesus died, so that he could take our sins away." She explained. "Who is Jesus?" I asked, "Jesus is God's son and before you ask me who God is. God is a spirit that we pray to and worship. We worship him once we know the truth. To do that you must first ask him to come into your life. You can receive him at any time because he stands at the door of your heart and knocks, and you have to be willing to let him in. Then you must find out what is pleasing to him." "Oh!" I exclaimed, "now I understand what the man, I mean preacher meant when he said ask and you shall receive, seek and you shall find, knock and it will open." Surprised, big mama said, "how did you remember that?" "I meditated, when you told me to be quiet in church this morning. Meditate baby, the word is meditated." "Meditate" I said, and I memorized it to! "Tell me more about Jesus, God's son and where he is?" I asked. Just then, my mother called me to get ready for bed.

"Oh! Momma! Please! Not now big mama hasn't finished her story." I pleaded. "Well, she's just going to have to finish it upstairs. You're going to have to start practicing going to bed early so when school starts in the fall you will be ready." Big mama rose from the swing and grabbed my hand ever so tightly, which meant shutting your mouth and let's go.

Big mama had never put us to bed before, that was always my mother's job. So upstairs, we went, and she pulled out my nightclothes and my little sisters too. We undressed and dressed for bed. Then we both declared the head of the bed even though we knew someone had to have the foot. So, we raced to jump in the bed. Suddenly big mama said, "You all just might as well stop and kneel down and say your prayers tonight before anybody goes to sleep." "What are prayers?" Ladybug asked. "Prayers are words to God." I explained. "Who is God?" She asked. "He's a spirit and we worship him in spirit and in truth." I proudly explained. "Very good, I'm so very proud of you for remembering that." Big mama was grinning from ear to ear. "Oh, don't you worry. I promise you I will always remember everything you tell me because I got my recorder on." She couldn't help but laugh and she drew me close.

She placed a pillow on the floor, knelt down beside the bed and we joined her. Big mama had a look of confusion on her face. "Tell me don't you girls kneel down on your knees at night before you get in bed." She asked us "No, came the reply. "Tell me, does your mother put you to bed every night?" "No!" said ladybug "she says get you damn clothes off and get in the bed right now!" "That's a bad word, don't say that again do you hear me!" Big mama demanded. "Yes, I'm sorry!" She said. "That's a sin!" I said.

"Okay we are going to learn to say a little prayer. Now listen. Now I lay me down to sleep I pray the Lord my soul to keep if I should die before I wake, I pray the Lord my soul to take this I ask in Jesus' name amen." We prayed the prayer again after big mama and she hugged and kissed us and tucked us in bed.

"Emma Mae!" I heard big mama calling my mother as she left the room. "Why have you not taught the girls to pray?" "They are too young." She said. "No, they are not. This is the time in their lives you need to start them so that when they get older, they'll know." "Well, you have my permission to start them then cause I have too many things to do." My momma replied. "Like what? What could be so very important that you can't teach your children? Drinking, partying or running the streets? What could be so important?" Questioned big mama. Momma was silent "Emma Mae baby if you train these children now when you need them, they will be there." Big mama said sweetly but in a stern and authoritative voice. "Yeah, Yeah I hear you I've got to go. Thanks for putting the kids to bed. I will see you later." Momma said. I could hear the side door shut and then silence.

I knew momma was going out, tonight was Sunday, but I still overheard momma talking about going out. But it didn't matter because I knew big mama was going to be there. She was never going to leave us.

It seemed like forever before I heard big mama come upstairs. So, I pretended to need to use the bathroom so I could talk to her one more time before I went to sleep. "Where are you going?" asked ladybug "To the bathroom! Go to sleep!" I said. "Well hurry back before my feet get cold!" she said.

Big mama was in the hallway, and she turned to see me coming out of the door. "Where are you trying to go?" She asked. "To the bathroom." I answered. "Well, you had better hurry up before your feet get cold. Don't nobody want you to sleep with them with no cold feet." She laughed as she spoke. I rushed past her to the bathroom and finished quickly. She was still in the hall looking out the window humming when I came back out of the bathroom. "Are you going to bed?" I asked. "Yes, but first I got to steal away and pray." Big mama responded. "I thought stealing was a sin?" I asked with a puzzled look on my face. "It sure is, but what I mean by stealing away to pray is to stop doing whatever I'm doing and go somewhere where there is nobody but me and the Lord and I can pray and talk to him, and he can speak to me." She explained. "Come on and let me put you back in bed." Once she placed the covers over me, she walked over to the big rocking chair, pulled up to the potbelly stove, put covers over her shoulders and began to rock.

Everyone now was sleep but me, and she knew it. "Baby sister, do you know why I tell you pray every day?" She asked. "No! Not really." I answered. "Well, she said, the key to survival is prayer and to pray daily is the answer to all your needs being met. When I was a little girl around your age, in the old days when people had just been released from slavery and they had us sharecropping to survive. I just believed that God could hear my prayers for real freedom. God told me I would be a free woman one-day I would be able to make my own living and see my family grow and prosper and anything I wanted I could have if I just had faith and believed. God makes a way out of nothing. I have seen five generations living right now in my family. We don't have much compared to man's standards, but we are rich according to God. God loves us and wants us to trust him to give us what we need. Well, that is a story for another day, you just go to sleep. I have got a lot on my mind right now and I need to pray. Good night and God bless you baby." She whispered. "May God bless you too and I love you too big mama." I whispered back.

I must have thought about what big mama said until I fell off to sleep. I wondered why God would not give us much if we asked him, looked for him and opened the door for him to come in. If he made everything and everything belonged to him, why is it, we didn't have much? But I believed in my big mama. It might not be clear as to what God would do, or if we would ever get much more. But if big mama said we were to ask and pray for anything we wanted and believe God would provide it. As big mama would say "You will understand it better by and by."

CHAPTER 2

Train Up A Child

Proverbs 22:6
Train up a child in the way he should go, and when
he is old he will not depart from it.

"No, absolutely not! Last Sunday she came home. Her little hands and feet were cold. All y'all got is a potbelly stove and God knows how many people trying to gather round it. My baby doesn't need to go to church every time the door swings open, let her stay right here where she can be safe and warm." I heard my mom saying.

"Big mama, big mama please I want to go!" I pleaded. I had been ease dropping in the hall again and before I knew it, I was in the living room pleading with my case. "Momma please let me go I'll be warm and big mama I'll be good. Please let me go?" I looked at my mom and smiled. That half-grin warmed my momma's heart and that glaze in my eyes led my great-great-grandmother to take the authority position.

"Now listen and hear me good Emma Mae! If you raise up a child the way he should go, when he gets old, he won't depart from it." Big mama said stroking my hair. I knew right then I was going cause my mother just hated when big mama quoted scripture, she said she could never win, and she would rather have a beaten than to listen to her preach. So momma just gave in. "Okay Clemmy! But if she gets sick then you are the one that has to take care of her." She snapped. "Okay go put on your Sunday dress, stockings, your pants underneath and then boots and gloves and come on here." Instructed big mama. "Hurry up, your big mama is waiting." My momma chanted. I rushed off to get ready and I felt victorious.

We must have walked what seemed like a mile in the snow and big mama rubbed my hands ever so often. When we arrived at the church there were already some folks there and it wasn't long before they started to get loud. Then the preacher said everyone give a scripture. When it was my turn big mama leaned over and whispered in my ear "Jesus wept." I repeated it. It seemed like we were there all day and finally, it was time to go home. Big mama and I walked back, and I asked her what does Jesus wept mean?

"Jesus cried." She said "Why? Why did Jesus' cry? Did something bad happen, did someone die?" I questioned. "Yes baby, his friend died, and he was sad because he loved him so." She explained. "Well why did he die? Was he sick? Did he get killed?" I asked. "I don't know." Big mama answered. "Well why do people die? Will we see them again? Where do they go?" I asked. "Slow down baby girl I can't answer but one question at a time. Everybody must die and where he or she goes depends on if they live like Jesus or the Devil." I interrupted I know who Jesus is, that's God's son that cried right the one we go to church to praise right?" I asked. "Yes honey." She replied. "Well, who is the devil?" "The devil is Jesus' enemy; he is bad and makes people do and say bad things to hurt other people's feelings or do them harm. He comes to destroy families and put children against parents and all kinds of awful things. Baby girl, make sure you understand me cause the devil is sly like a fox." "Oh yeah I think I know. It's like when Flip Wilson says the devil made me do it." I said. "Sort of but you'll understand it better by and by." She said, smiling down at me. We walked quietly along, and she held my gloved hand ever so tightly and swung it a little to keep the blood running, as she liked to say.

Then a scary thought came to mind. "Big mama is you going to die?" I asked. "Yes, baby I am." She replied. "When?" I asked. "I don't know" she answered. "Are you going to live for Jesus or the devil?" I questioned. "I'm going to live with Jesus," she answered with a glow on her face, I will never forget. "Then me too" I said with conviction and pride. "Big mama!" I said sadly. "Yes baby." She answered. "I'm going to wept like Jesus when you die cause you're my friend and I love you." She got real quiet.

It started to snow with heavy wet flakes and big mama said we needed to pick up the pace. We finally arrived home. Big mama said, "Okay baby stop with the questions long enough to get off the wet clothes and get dried up. As she wiped me dry with the towel. "Achue!" I sneezed. "God bless you!" Replied, big mama. "Achue!" I sneezed again. "Clemmy!" My mom rushed in the room shouting. "See there that child has caught a death of cold already." Moving big mama to the side and taking the towel out of her hand. "I guess you just won't be satisfied until she dies?" She said hatefully. "Oh, momma don't worry about me if I die, I'm going to live with Jesus not the devil because I'm not going to let the devil make me do it!" I blurted. Big mama winked from her new position on the couch and a big, weird smile came on my momma's face. "Well Clemmy she sure enough is yours." Big mama now was beaming with delight and grinning with a full smile. "I know that's the one I told you when she was born in this world that's the one." Big mama confirmed. Well, I just couldn't figure out what all of that meant but I knew one thing. I would understand it better by and by.

It must have snowed the entire winter. Every Sunday it was either too cold or too snowy for me to go to church with big mama. She wasn't taking any chances with my health and momma was letting her. So I stayed at home and had fun playing cards and keeping secrets from big mama like the grownups and the older children played cards and Pokeno while she went to church. Big mama never asked me to tell her anything she always just knew so she freed me from thinking I was a tattle tell or a bad secret bearer. She would always just end her prayers with "God save my household from sinning in the flesh and draw them away from sinful thoughts and deeds." She would always say, "Lord you know their sins better than I do so I don't have to call them out. Please deliver them from yielding to the devil's influence."

Well, the snow and the cold just keep coming before the snow melts from one big snow another would come and close down the schools and make the roads impassable. But one particular Sunday in January we had a bright and sunny morning. The weatherman said that it was going to warm up and then a blizzard would hit before evening. I was strong and healthy, and I longed to go and fellowship with the saints, so I begged my momma to let me go with big mama to church. Momma was really skeptical. She asked big mama, who by the way was a pretty good weather predictor, if she thought that it would snow before we finished church. Big mama said it was God's business to conduct the weather in whatever way he wanted and that if we were to have a blizzard then the best place would be in the house of God shut in to pray. Well momma still was not convinced but then big mama said that if it did keep us from coming home not to worry everything that was ever needed for man's survival could be found worshipping God. Then she looked at me and said, "Now go get dressed and come on." I flew up the steps and got dressed.

When I returned, Vandy was making excuses as to why he wasn't able to walk us to church. His head hurt, his nose was stopped up and his back hurt from shoveling snow. Big mama told him it was all right and not to come running when it started snowing trying to rush her home we would be shut in for the long haul and then she smiled and winked at me. Momma said, "Well I know you have got a plan so take my baby and y'all head to church before I change my mind." Vandy told me I was a brave solider and that he respected me for that. Then he kissed me on the cheek, hugged my neck and asked me to say a prayer or two for him.

Big Mama had picked up her big purse today that was always an indication that she expected something to happen. Momma teased her about the big purse, she said she had everything in it except the kitchen sink. When I would try and pick it up it felt like she had packed that in there too. But big mama didn't care how much anyone teased her she had a survival kit and goodies in that purse, and as heavy as it was it never slowed her down.

We walked swiftly down the old school yard, down to Jones Street then to Bland Street as we turned the corner to Genoa Avenue the first snowflakes started to fall. They were soft and wet to me, but big mama said they were heavy and that was an indication that they were ready for an all-night prayer service. She said, "I can feel it down in my soul and in my bones too." She made a face as if she were in pain but smiling, nonetheless. Pastor Blaine met us at the door. "What brave warriors I have in you two ladies. Rev. Hairston, now I know you know that the weatherman called for a blizzard tonight ain't nobody in here driving so maybe if you want to you should turn around now and get home before the real snow comes." "Thank you kindly, but no thank you!" She said as she hugged his neck and peeked inside to see who had shown up. We hadn't been inside long before two deacons, Mrs. Collie and the tambourine lady came. Then the piano man showed up and then Mr. and Mrs. Cato. Pastor Blaine welcomed everyone and explained to us that the weatherman had called for a blizzard and that because no one had a car, he would excuse anyone that wanted to leave. Nobody took him up on his offer. Mrs. Collie asked him did we still have food in the kitchen and was it enough dry wood and coal to keep the fires going. The deacons said that they would make sure of that while we got service started. They disappeared out into the backroom and the Pastor went to the pulpit. He prayed that God's will be done in God's church today that if God saw fit for us to leave or stay then God would provide all of our needs. Then he started service. The deacons reappeared with their overcoats full of snow. Pastor Blaine asked them what they thought and on one accord they replied, "Shut in!"

It was a very unusual service from the very beginning the pianist started to play and Mr. and Mrs. Cato started to sing, I couldn't lift my head. It was like God was standing right in the midst of the room and I wouldn't dare look up at him. I don't know how the other people felt because I was afraid to look around the room. It was so peaceful, and then I got all warm and happy inside. All I could hear was say yes. Say yes. I started quietly saying yes and then yes Lord and then I got louder. Well, I must have stirred up something because the pianist got the spirit, the tambourine lady got to playing double time and I got to shouting. I shouted in the corner for a long time. Finally, I ran into the wall and one of the deacons came over and asked me was I all right. Then he told me to watch as well as pray then I shouted some more. We must have sung five or six songs before it finally calmed down enough for us to take a seat. I looked around for big mama and she was sprawled face down at the altar speaking to God in her secret heavenly language.

Momma and her friends had a secret language they would speak when they didn't want us children to know what they were talking about, they called it Pig Latin. Big mama said that she spoke in tongue, and it was called a heavenly language. It was unique to every individual and that only God could understand it. That is unless God wanted someone to translate it for the church. It was her private way of conversing with God. I wanted my own private language too, but big mama said, don't play with the spirit of the living God. When God was ready to give me my own language and to privately speak to me then He would. Until then don't mock nobody for that would make God angry and He wasn't very nice when He got angry. So I feared the Lord and dare not play with the special things of God. Then I started to wonder was I really shouting or was I mocking. I had never felt like fire was shut up in my bones before, even though I had heard the story many times before. But today I had fire all over me and I wasn't alone. Pastor Blaine preached like a dying man on death row. He poured out his heart through the word of God as he preached about Goodness and Mercy and they sure enough were about to be displayed up in this house.

Church was over today faster than it had ever been, I looked up at the clock in the corner and sure enough it was 3:00 p.m. already. Pastor Blaine asked to prepare the church for a shut in that the snow was already up to the steps, the streets were covered, and it was still coming down. Mrs. Collie headed for the kitchen. The deacons stirred up the coals in the potbelly stove and went to check on the stove in the kitchen. Big mama went to the closet and pulled out blankets and handed them to Mrs. Cato. She smiled and asked me would I like to join the Ministry of Helps Club. I didn't understand what they were doing but I wanted to be a part of it, so I said yes. She asked me to go and count the people. I went into the kitchen and through the chapel counting people. There were ten so I reported my count and then went to the window to look out. It was truly beautiful, bright, and a huge accumulation of snow. I wondered how many snowflakes God had to send to make that much snow and did he have to count them. I stood at the window daydreaming when I heard big mama interrupting my thoughts. "You said ten?" "Yes ten." I replied. Then I continued wondering how were we going to get home? If the snow was over my head who would carry me? Big mama knew my mind was a big snowdrift at that moment, so she invited me to rejoin them in the ministry of helps saying once I put my hand to the plow there was no room for turning back. So I resumed my chore and asked what was next. "Good, now go over there and count the blankets as you place them on the chairs in the corner. I never counted pass ten before so when I got to ten big mama, and sister Cato helped me I made twenty trips to the chairs carrying blankets. Big mama said everyone would get two apiece if they needed them if not, they would still be available. It wasn't long before Mrs. Collie came out the kitchen sweating. "It's hot as a firecracker in there!" She said. "Well, I guess by now the snow done sealed up all the drafts, so we are going to be good and toasty in here. Pastor Blaine said. Everyone started to laugh, and I did too. I pictured myself looking like a piece of toast with apple butter.

Big mama and Mrs. Cato headed for the kitchen, and I was hot on their heels. I had never been inside the kitchen before, it was huge. It had a large table with nice chairs, a tablecloth and candles. Mrs. Cato said she would check the cabinets for more matches and candles. The deacons filled pots and jugs with water from the sink. They placed them on the counters, in the corners of the kitchen floor and everywhere there was space for an empty jug to be filled and placed. Big mama said she would set the table for dining. She used that word when she wanted everything in the kitchen to be picture perfect.

"You know baby sister there is no place better to be than in the house of God dining at his table. The Bible says that the Lord has many feasts, and he prepares a table before us in the presence of our enemies. Today is what God has allowed us to see. He makes the weather and grants us the privilege to see every season, although too much of a good thing can be bad for you!" She chuckled. "But laying all jokes aside we can rest assured that God works all things together for his good." Amen chimed in the tambourine lady as she joined us in the kitchen. Then they all laughed. I wasn't quite sure what she meant.

Snow was bad for me altogether. It kept me from going outside, from being with my friends, going to school, going to church and now from going home. So, if it meant that we had to be snowed in at the church and big mama was going to be chewed out by my momma when she got us home then it was bad. But if it meant that I would be beside my big mama in the house of the Lord praying all night long with the saints of God then it was good.

Pastor Blaine joined us in the kitchen along with the other deacons and they were all smiles. "Bless the Lord! Bless the Lord. I smell Chef Collie's cooking up in here! What are you whipping up in here." Exclaimed, Pastor Blaine. "Some tatter soup, cornbread and some fat back for tonight and tomorrow. I'm getting my menu planned out now, so I need to take out some meat from the freezer a little later on if God leads so we be fine tomorrow too." Sister Collie was just beaming, glad to be of service to God's people anyway she could. "Yes, mama Pastor Blaine said we could sure enough feast tonight and pray and fast tomorrow if we run out of food. You ever fasted before?" He asked me. "Fast? What's a fast I asked him?" "Well child that's when you turn down your plate and don't have nothing to eat from one mealtime to the next." He explained. "Well, I can't rightly say I have Pastor Blaine, but we been short on food does that count?" I asked. "Only if you prayed child only if you prayed!' He said smiling and chuckling.

The table was set, and the deacons had made sure all the chairs were in place. They had placed a milk carton case on one of the chairs for me next to big mama so that I could fit at the table. Pastor blessed the food and Mrs. Collie set the food on the table and everyone served themselves. Big mama fixed my plate.

As they talked and ate, I wondered. I believe I had fasted before I remember praying for food when we didn't have any and God sent some really late at night one time. "Yeah, I had fasted and if it ever got to be my turn to talk again, I was going to share my testimony.

When dinner was finished, I helped clean the dishes and put the leftover food up for late night snack if needed. That was what big mama called wrapping the food loosely in wax paper and setting it in the refrigerator. Pastor Blaine announced that we needed to set the church up for evening and all-night service. He explained that the chairs were to be put in the aisle in the center of the church where they would be out of the way of those wanting to praise all night and those wanting to sleep. It was my opportunity to stay up all night until morning light if I wanted to big mama said. As long as I was praying, singing or meditating on God. It sounded exciting.

We started the service again and again pastor opened the door for testimony service, and I was the second one to testify. I told them that I wanted to thank God for giving me a chance to fast. I remembered that we didn't have any food in our house all day long one day and I prayed that God would send us some food and when it was after dark, momma came back home with some souse meat. I hated souse meat, and I remember saying that I wasn't going to ask God's blessing over no souse meat. So, while everybody else was praying I never mumbled a word. I ate one piece of souse meat and about three crackers. Then I asked to be excused. When I got upstairs, I told my big mama what I had done. She told me I was being ungrateful and regardless of whether I was satisfied with God's blessing or not I should have blessed his name. She told me that in the days of old, many died because of ungratefulness. The next morning, I woke up sick on my stomach. I prayed. "God please don't let me die and forgive me for not being grateful for blessing me with something to eat last night when we didn't have anything else. After I had thrown up about three times God sent my momma upstairs with some homemade chicken noodle soup, a thermometer, some cod liver oil and extra blanket. I testify to the saints of God today that the Lord is merciful, kind and forgiving. Pray much for me as I grow to appreciate the things of God and learn how to live like my big mama says Holy.

The church was so quiet and only the piano man was playing softly. I looked over at the deacons and they were covering their faces with their gloved hands. I looked towards where Mr. & Mrs. Cato and the tambourine lady were sitting and they all looked as though they were sleeping, their eyes were closed but tears were streaming down their cheeks. It stayed that way for a good long time before Pastor spoke and then all he could say was out of the mouth of babes and suck lings thou have perfected praise. I didn't understand what he meant but big mama always said, "You will understand it better by and by."

The service continued all night long and I could see through the window that it had not ceased snowing either. I could hear the wind howling, and shaking the window. The more it howled the more piano man played. When the window shook the Cato's sang like bluebirds on a beautiful spring day that had just feed their newborn babies. To me it sounded like everything God created was now praising him in its own way. The windows shook to the beat. The wind howled a soft Hallelujah giving God praise and the saints of God were singing, shouting and praying. Big mama was right. There really wasn't anything more special than my church family.

I was the baby of the church and Pastor Blaine asked everyone to take turns and pray. They let me have my turn and I experienced something I will never forget. Just a closer walk with thee was playing softly in the background and I began to pray the way I saw big mama do I knelt at the altar and opened my mouth to ask God's cleansing and blessing. But when I realized where I was, I was over by my special wall the one I bumped into earlier shouting and praising God. I don't know what happened. All I know is that everyone and I mean everyone was shouting all over the church. Funniest thing nobody ever bumped into the potbelly stove that was in the center of the church.

When the long hand got on the twelve and the shorthand was on the ten. Pastor Blaine stopped to assign prayer warriors one hour each throughout the night. I didn't have a turn, so I keep watch with big mama who was the oldest and was asked to go first. I knelt by her side at the altar and prayed with her for one hour. I must have said amen a hundred times thinking that she was through to find out she was only scratching the surface. I never knew there was so much to pray for Rev. Dr. Martin Luther King Jr., schools, schoolteachers, firemen, police, presidents, pastors all over the world, sick people, hospitals, mental illness, poor people, rich people you name it big mama prayed for it. When Mrs. Cato tapped her on the shoulder to signal that she was taking over, I had to help Mrs. Cato help her up so that she could sit down, she looked tired, but she was glowing.

I was sleepy and when I was offered a chance to lie down, I took um up on it. I laid in the first set of chairs that were pulled together close to but far enough away from the stove to feel the heat and not get burnt. Big mama wrapped me up in one cover like a newborn baby tight and secure and then draped the other cover over me. The chair was not too bad as a matter of fact it was quite comfortable, and I was fast to sleep in no time flat.

I was awakened by the sound of a street scrapper. It was just outside the window, so I got up stretched and went over to the window to look out. The scrapper was throwing snow up against the church wall. I started to knock on the window and to tell him not to do that. He looked up and kept shoveling. Pastor Blaine came over to me and told me not to knock too hard on a cold and frozen glass it might break. "Sorry!" I said. He looked out to see that the scrapper had pushed the snow on the side of the building. It looked taller than my brother Vandy. "My goodness what snow we done had!" Pastor remarked. Mrs. Collie had already started fixing breakfast and big mama was praying. I wondered did she ever go to sleep when I went to sleep, she was ready to go back to the altar. Knowing her she probably did do all night prayer. When she heard me stirring around, she said amen and came to hug my neck and get me ready for the new day. "Baby sister, come on let's go to the bathroom and get fresh." She went to the corner and picked up her purse. We went off to the bathroom. In the bathroom she pulled out a washcloth, a bar of homemade soap, towel, clean underwear and a clean tee shirt. She put the stopper in the sink and told me to sit on the commode while she went to get the hot water. It was cold in the bathroom, and I wished she would hurry up and return. She returned as quickly as she could and filled the basin full of warm water and I quickly washed up and put on clean underwear and the same top clothes I had on the day we arrived.

We ate and started to sing and praise God some more. The Cato's sang like they were renewed and regenerated from resting peacefully all night long, piano man played ever so sweetly, and the tambourine lady tapped softly as if she could do another hour of sleep before she was ready to praise. Nevertheless, the praises continued, and I was happy to be in the number one more time.

We praised and worshipped for what appeared to be hours before a stranger opened the church door and slide through. "Pardon me people of God. I just want to ask you a question. Do you know there is another blizzard forecasted for tonight?" Pastor Blaine looked at everyone in the room and everyone shook their heads no. "Well! If you don't mind, I have a suggestion. I work for the city. I have a this here snowplow outside and I have finished cleaning the main roads and I am about to plow the side streets, if you would like I can take some of you home as I clean the street. Now I might not be able to get you to your doorsteps, but I can get you close. It's a prediction of freezing weather tonight and some pipes might burst if nobody is home to take care of them so how bout if I take you people home?"

Well, it must have been a messenger from God sending his angel just for me cause I wanted to go home, and I just wanted big mama to go too. "Well," Pastor looked around and said "We know that God is well pleased with our service in His house, now it is time to make sure our other homes that God has given to us are secure. God wants us to be good stewards over everything he gives us so pack up and let's get to getting it." It was like a sigh of relief fell over the people. They started cleaning, packing and gathering up stuff. The stranger went around the room asking people where they lived, and he made out a plan to get everyone home. Pastor, big mama and I were the last because we lived up the main street.

It was clean, and he just had to clean the side streets to get us to our houses.

Several hours went by and I thought the stranger had forgotten us when finally, he returned looking worn out and cold. So big mama made him a cup of hot chocolate and let him warm himself by the potbellied stove while pastor gathered the water jugs, some firewood and coal and placed several boxes on the back of the truck. We prayed and left the church. The scraper had no problem going up Bland Street but when we turned on to Jones Street it was foot upon foot of snow. Only a path where children had made to ride sleds was visible, "My God I had no idea that much snow had fallen," said big mama. "Me neither!" said Pastor Blaine in astonishment. "Well, the weatherman is calling for about the same amount again tonight along with freezing cold, so I know you'll need to be home with your families, so they don't worry." Said the stranger. "Well, we can't thank you enough!" Pastor and big mama said together. "Well if you think about it, can you just be praying for my family? They are always worried about me out here on these dangerous roads all times of the day and night, but a man's got to do what a man's got to do to keep his family feed and clothed. If you know what I mean." Said the stranger. "Certainly!" Pastor said. He plowed the street picture perfect laying the snow to the side and keeping a nice smooth path up the middle. Said if I decided later to go sleigh riding, I would have nice smooth sailing just as long as I was a good driver and stayed in the middle. When we reached the playground, he said he couldn't go up the schoolyard it was against his rules, so he blew his horn and Pastor helped big mama out of the truck and then me. He picked up several of the boxes, several bags that the blankets were in and about five jugs of water and sat them in the snow. Vandy must have known it was big mama, because I saw him coming as soon as we got out of the truck.

We thanked the man and just like he appeared, he suddenly turned the truck around and disappeared. He had just gotten out of sight when the snow started to fall. Several of the men in the neighborhood came outside still bucking boots and pulling overcoats on with shovels in their hands. Vandy kissed big mama on the cheek and told her how worried he was and how much he missed us. Shovels started moving and the path was blazed from one end of the schoolyard to the house which by the way, Vandy had already shoveled a path from the end of the yard up the steps to our house in expectation of our arrival.

The boxes and bags must have been stuffed with goodies and necessities because all I could hear coming from the kitchen was thank you Jesus from momma and big mama as they unpacked, and I undressed and warmed by our coal stove.

I prayed hard that night the windows rattled as if they would break, and the snow keep pouring bucket after bucket and it was a race to plug up any new holes that snow would come in when you noticed it. But for some reason it wasn't too unbearably cold. Momma made hot pudding for dessert and big mama stayed downstairs past her bedtime just so we could all cuddle, talk and yes pray. It was a night

I will never forget a record four foot ten inches of snow with ten-foot snowdrifts.

A family warm and together thanks to stranger who provided us with a ride home, a pastor that put extra coal, wood, blankets and food in boxes and bags for us to enjoy and a big mama that knew how to pray and get God's favor. I didn't quite understand everything that had happened, but as big mama liked to say, "You will understand it even better by and by."

CHAPTER 3

Have Faith As A Mustard Seed

Matthew 17:20a
If you have faith as a mustard seed you will say to this
mountain, "Move from here to there, and it will move; and
nothing will be impossible for you."

In the spring of the year, it is a time of newness of joy. Everything starts new and you have a chance to change your old habits and do something new. If you have been doing badly you can do good. If you are wrong, you can go right. Whatever you need to change spring is time. Now that's what my big mama use to say.

I loved the spring, the flowers bursting out with blooms and the trees and their different blossoms. The blue birds, the red birds singing and nesting in the trees. The walks that big mama and I used to take as she explained life and nature the best she could were best times of my life.

Now big mama was a large woman. She must have been in her late eighties, so walking with her was always slow and enjoyable because she would stop and rest and show me something I had never seen.

"Big mama, where does all this nature stuff come from? I asked. "It's God's handiwork." She replied. "Remember I told you God owns everything, and he made everything, and he knows everything." Then suddenly she said, "Shh! See look over there in the trees. She pointed to the shoemaker tree. Do you see the cardinal?" She asked. "Yeah, looks like he's looking for something to eat. You got anymore cornbread left?" I asked. "Yes baby." She whispered. "Well give it to me and I'll just run over there and feed him." I said holding out my hand. "No baby, he is not going to let you get close enough to feed him just throw it on the ground and be quiet he'll come and get it." I did as she instructed. Then she pointed to a nice big tree stump, and said, "Let's sit over there and watch." I loved this time more than anything in life. I loved it because it was my time alone with big mama and I knew she was going to tell me something nobody else knew. We walked over to the tree stump, and it had enough room for both of us so instead of sitting on her lap, I sat beside her like a big girl.

"God knows that the birds have to eat and that's his job to feed them and He takes good care of them. Just like the birds, He takes care of us. For He knows what we have need of even before we ask. We have to ask God for things because he wants to hear from us. That's why I tell you every night to kneel and pray. That's how you talk to God. You don't have to let nobody hear you pray because God sees your heart. He knows your thoughts, and he feels your pain, so you really don't have to pray out loud. Sometimes you just meditate." Big mama was so good at telling stories, I was waiting for her to tell me one, but she sat there quietly almost like she was asleep but her eyes were open.

"Big mama when it was cold this winter, I prayed for another cover. Then when we were hungry and there was only one sandwich apiece, I prayed for more food, but God didn't give me no more cover or no more sandwiches. I guess God didn't answer because momma wouldn't let me get on the floor on my knees like you do." I said sadly. "Well baby let me ask you something. Did you freeze to death? Did you starve to death?" Questioned big mama. "No, but I was cold and hungry." I replied, "But you had some cover, and you had some food, right?" She asked in a gentle voice. "Yes." I replied. "Then just remember this. God supplies your need. It may not always be the way you want it or all that you want but he supplies your need. If you are grateful for the little things and continue to love God even when you don't see him doing nothing, you will be faithful, and God is pleased with faithfulness." She got quiet again. "Okay I will remember that I got my recorder on." I said smiling up at her.

"Shh! Look over there." She pointed. The bird had come down and swooped a big chunk of cornbread and flew up in the tree to a nest. "He's gone to feed his family. It ain't nothing like having family and taking care of it. Family should always come first." She said.

"Big mama I thought you said it was God's job to feed the birds? That bird is eating the cornbread I put over there. Why didn't God come down here and feed the bird?" "Well, child, God sent you and me out here to do his work. God lives in Heaven and He just don't come down here to do things like that. He uses people who are already down here and available. He can send you to a place without you even knowing why and use you to do the job he wants done. Just don't question God do all you can when you see a need so that God will be pleased." "You might not understand it now but you will understand it better by and by." She said smiling. "Okay" I said as 1 paused to think of another question.

"Big Mama why is it you and momma are always fussing? Don't you love each other?" I asked. "Why of course we love each other sometimes people don't always see eye to eye on certain things, but it doesn't mean that they don't love each other. You know, your mother just needs to draw close to God. I know she knows him. I want her to and in time she will cause you're going to lead her right?" She smiled. "Anything you say. Big mama I love you." I said. "And I love you too. Now help me up off this stump and let's get to heading home." She replied.

As we walked slowly down the road big mama held my hand securely and rubbed it ever so gently and swung my arm until a big wide grin broaden my face. I looked up at her and she was smiling back at me. "Now that's the smile I love to see, that's the one everyone says belongs to me." Beaming I knew just what she meant because everybody said I looked like, acted like and talked like Clemmy and that's what they called me most of the time "Little Clemmy".

CHAPTER 4

You Got To Live In This World

John 15:19
If you were of the world, the world would love its own. Yet, because you are not in the world, but I chose you out of the world, therefore the world hates you.

"Baby sister, wake up, get up." came the voice of big mama. "Come on baby girl I want you to get ready. Today is the big day!" She was so excited she sounded like she was singing the words. "Big day for what?" I asked. "The first day of school!" She replied as I rolled out the bed. "Well then get ladybug up too!" I said longing for the bed and rubbing sleep out of my eyes. "No baby she's not old enough yet in time you will all be going and you get a chance to be her big sister and teach her the ropes. But right now, it's your turn." Big mama said as she hugged me. I looked at the bed I had just gotten out of and watched ladybug still sleeping snug as a bug in a rug and I smiled to myself.

Big mama was already fully dressed and had the ironing board close to the potbelly stove. The iron was heating up and I saw the prettiest dress on the ironing board I had ever seen, and it looked to be my size. "Big mama what is school like?" I asked. "Baby girl I don't know I never went but when you get home you are going to tell me all about it right?" She asked smiling down at me. "Sure, I promise!" I answered. "Here take this washcloth and go over to the table and wash your face, hands and hind parts. Don't put no whole lot of soap on the rag either, just enough to wash off, you know how to do it." She instructed. "Okay but I got to pee first." I replied. "Now is that what you're going to say in school today?" She asked. "Yes." I said. "Well, I think it would sound better if Camilla Garnet would say. Can I use the bathroom, please?" She corrected. As I headed for the door I jokingly said, "Well if Camilla Garnet has to use the bathroom, she had better be quicker than me cause, baby sister got to pee first." I quickly ran to the bathroom, finished my business and returned.

The pan of water was still hot, and it felt so very good to my face. I thanked God for hot water because it made me feel brand new. When I had finished washing up, big mama had finished pressing the dress. It was so pretty, and it was so neat. I asked, "Is it mine?" "Yes, what other little girl in this room could fit this dress. Now look right over there under that chair and get them other clothes and hurry up. You've got to eat breakfast before the bus comes." She said. "Bus? I'm riding a bus?" I asked. "Yes, now please baby sister don't start with the questions just do what I ask you to." She said sternly.

I went to the chair and found new underwear, new socks, and under the chair new shoes. Boy was I ever excited. "Is this mine? Big mama are these shoes mine?" "Yes, now hurry baby!" I dressed ever so quickly and when I had put on my underclothes and my old slip big mama said, "Now put on this T-shirt and go downstairs, your mother has breakfast ready for you." "But what about my dress, I can't wear my new dress to school." I whined. "Baby sister, do you think I'm going to let you out of this house in a T-shirt?" We both laughed. "Big mama, I love you. Thank you for my clothes." I said. "You are welcome, but you have to thank God for them. It was only by his grace and mercy you got them." Okay, I will, where is He?" I said trying to make a joke. But big mama wasn't about any jokes with God. "Now just because you big enough to go out to school don't start acting new on God you know where to find him." She said in her authoritative voice.

Just then my mother called up the steps, "Baby sister come down here and get your breakfast before I feed it to the dogs." We ain't have no dogs and I knew that's what momma always said when she cooked and had to wait for someone longer than she wanted too.

"See you taken to long you know your mother is short on patience so stop playing and don't get on her nerves." "Okay!" I promised. I went downstairs and momma had cream of wheat and toast, just the way I like it. It was so good. When I had finished big mama was right there taking off my T-shirt putting on my dress and combing my hair at the same time. She was moving so fast; I thought I was a movie star being groomed for my next stage appearance like on TV. "You have such fine hair; it only needs brushing." Said big mama as she tied it up in two beautiful ponytails.

"Clemmy, you are bound and determined to spoil that poor child to death. She ain't going to be no good for nothing if you have your way." My momma said. "Oh, stop complaining Emma Mae I ain't hear you complain when I use to treat you like this. Now don't she look pretty, that's my baby. I'm so proud of you! And just in case you need some reassurance Emma Mae, I am proud of you too!" She said winking at me. Momma acted as though she was not paying big mama any attention, but I knew she liked to hear big mama say nice things to her, she said it to her all the time but mostly when momma was worried was when she said it the most.

"Come on here child. This came in the mail." My mother said as she pinned the plastic card onto my new dress and continued to talk to big mama. "Clemmy, I just don't understand what they are trying to do. I just don't like this. Dr. Martin Luther King Jr. and his non-violence movement done scared these white people to death. How they just going to on their own, call themselves, starting this new Head-start program. Busing my four-year-old way across town to test her like some guinea pig and if that don't beat all they won't let the parents come along with their children. I just ought to be mean and climb right up on that bus and go with my baby." My mama protested.

"Now Emma Mae fair exchange ain't never been no robbery. These children are young and fresh. Older folks tend to be set in their ways. If we are ever going to learn to get along, we got to start somewhere." She said defensively. "Well, it seems to me, you ought to be one of the last ones in favor of this integration stuff. You were around when slavery ended you know firsthand the treatment and cruelty white people can hand out. I just want my baby to be safe and it ain't no guarantee that she will be treated right out there at that school." My momma said.

"It ain't no guarantee she will be treated right at the school right down the street. Our own people are prejudice against each other. You just have to learn to trust God, and if God's name is in anything positive then say yeah and amen. If I spent my whole life mad at folks because they didn't treat me the way I thought they should, I would never be able to pray." Corrected big mama. "What's praying go to do with this?" Questioned momma. "A person can't pray straight and get close to God with hate, hurt and meanness in his heart Emma Mae. God wants us to live, forgive and think good of people. Life is too short to hold grudges, hate folks and think the worse about people all the time. People need to learn to turn everything over to God's capable hands. He knows best and what will be is already in His plans."

Turning to me, big mama said, "You have got to go catch the bus and you can't be late. You're going to be fine cause I got you all prayed over."

Just as I had finished hugging her and gathering my thoughts. Ladybug came down the steps crying. "I'm all by myself upstairs, where are you going?" she asked me. "Wait for me!" She hollered. "You can't go right now it's not your turn but when you get big like me you can okay." I tried to explain and trying to hold her hand at the same time. But she wasn't a bit happy about the fact I was leaving her, she jerked her hand away and said, "Well bye!" Turning to go into the living room. I went after her, I didn't want her to be mad at me. She was my best friend; we did everything together. My momma walked over to me and said, "Let's go you have got to go! She'll be just fine. Clemmy can you please take her back upstairs until I walk baby sister to the bus?" Momma asked. "Sure, but I got to get me some more sugar to hold me the rest of the day." I dropped my mother's hand and ran to hug big mama's waist as she bent and kissed me on the forehead. "Now scat and be on your best behavior." She commanded. I turned and ran back to my momma, and we turned and went out the kitchen door down the side steps to the old school yard to wait for the bus.

As soon as I saw James and Jasmine and a whole lot of other kids I got scared. "Where they come from?" I asked. "It's school time. Do you think you're going to school by yourself?" My momma jokingly asked. "I don't know I ain't never been. But I'll let you know when I get home. I'll tell you all about it." I replied. "I'm sure you will Miss Garnet every little detail. But you had better not be a smart aleck and make them smart aleck remarks in school. Do you understand me, Miss Garnet." She said in her mean voice. "Miss Garnet, why you call me Miss Garnet?" I asked. I guess we got distracted because just then the bus came and on it sat some more kids and in the window was picture of a big giraffe. It stopped and off stepped a man that didn't look like us and immediately I knew he was the bus driver.

"Good morning boys and girls please be quiet and listen carefully." He shouted. Everyone froze as it got so quiet you could hear a pin drop. This is your first day at the new school. This is the giraffe bus, and you will ride the giraffe bus to school and back. Remember to look for the giraffe in the window. Now all aboard!" He shouted. I hugged my mother. James and little man got on and I stepped on very proudly behind them but "almond boy" he started to cry, and his mother had to carry him on the bus. It was the biggest, prettiest, yellow bus I had ever seen.

We rode for a long, long time. I wanted to go to sleep but the girl next to me keep seeing something new out the window and saying look at this and look at that. She bothered me all the way to school, but it was kind of fun. Finally, we arrived at this great big brick school much, much bigger than the school in the old school yard. I had never seen a building that big. But I had never been to school before either. The bus stopped and the driver said we would all line up in one line and follow the teacher that came to get us.

We waited for a minute and then out came, a lady that said follow me. She was pretty and had a pretty smile, but she didn't look like any of us either and I knew she was the teacher. Once we got inside, she asked us to sit in a circle on the floor of this big room. "Hello boys and girls, my name is Mrs. White. Please listen carefully. I am going to call your name from this list and if you hear me call your name line up on this side of the room. This is Mrs. Walker, and she will call the children on her list. If you hear her call your name, please line up on the other side of the room. The room was full of children all around my age, nobody was crying, and nobody was talking. I believed it was because they were all scared like me. I had never been in a room with so many people that didn't look like me. These people had red hair, yellow hair, brown hair, black hair, and green eyes, blue eyes and some even had cat eyes. Everybody I had ever known until now looked alike at least where brown. These people were white, some red and some tan. I think every child was looking at another wondering the same thing. At least I hoped they were because I didn't want to be the only one in culture shock.

Mrs. White started her list and when she finished, I was still sitting on the floor. Mrs. Walker walked over and started to call the children on her list. She called Camilla Garnet twice. I remembered big mama called her name early this morning. I wondered how big mama knew she was going to be at my school. I guess the Holy Ghost told her. I started to smile, and I wanted to say Camilla Garnet went to pee. But I remembered what my mother said about me not being a smart aleck in school, so I didn't want to make her mad. I sat with my mouth shut grinning. After she finished her list there were quite a few children still sitting on the floor. Only ones I knew were me, almond boy and little man and two girls I had seen but didn't remember their names.

Mrs. Walker came over and asked us what our names were. I said, "My name is baby sister but most of the time they call me little Clemmy," I was proud of my name. "Well, dear you have a real name because baby sister is just a nickname. Could your name be Camilla Garnet?" She said ever so sweetly. "It could be," I said, "my mother called me Miss Garnet this morning." I replied, "That is also what your nametag says." She said as she stretched out her hand to help me off the floor. She led me to her side of the room. Later she returned with little man, we both smiled. Little man said, "My name was William Mason. What's yours, Camilla Garnet?" and we both laughed. We were in Mrs. Walker's class. She took us up a flight of stairs to a nice big room with carpet on the floor, pictures on the wall, a big blackboard and lots of toys in a fenced corner. "Wow! This is great, look at all these toys." I said as I headed for them. "Wait a minute, Camilla. There is a special time in school we have set aside playing with the toys, but right now is not the time so please get back in line." I eased back in line. The room was full of small chairs, just my size and she told everyone to find a seat. I grabbed William's hand, and he said, "You going to sit by me? I don't know these other children and I don't trust them they look funny." "Well if you don't trust them I don't either. Sit close." I replied. We found two seats together and sat down.

Mrs. Walker started talking and she talked and talked. I tried to listen, but I couldn't wait to play with the toys. I kept looking over in the corner and hoping now was the time to play with them. But she kept talking, then I heard Mrs. Walker say, "Camilla, would you like to hold the flag?" "Sure!" I said and stood up. "Come stand beside me." She continued to talk. "This is the flag of the United States of America. It is very important. Hold it high." She said I raised it up over my head. "Bring it down just a little." She said and I did. She continued, "The flag represents everything our forefathers fought and died in wars for, so that this country could be free. You will respect the flag and salute it every day by learning and saying the Pledge of Allegiance. Everyone stands and face me raise your right hand." There was another lady in the room that looked like us that was walking around putting people's arms down and lifting the right one. Once she finished. Mrs. Walker said, "now take that hand and place it over your heart like this," and she showed us by turning around facing the same way we were. "Remember which hand you are using. Now say what I say. 'I pledge allegiance to the flag of the United States of America and to the republic for which it stands one nation under God indivisible with liberty and justice for all.'" I said, "Yeah and Amen really loud and all the children laughed but I didn't care because big mama would say that if God were in it say, Yeah and amen! "We will memorize or remember those words because we will say them every day." She smiled ever so sweetly. "Now thank you Camilla, you may take your seat." As she took the flag out of my hands. As I headed for my seat Mrs. Walker said, "Now children we are going to pray. " I knelt down by my seat and folded my hands, bowed my head and closed my eyes. "Camilla, we don't have to get on the floor to pray. That is good training but in school we just stand quietly, beside our chairs." So, I got up and stood by my chair and closed my eyes. She asked all the children to stand. She prayed a quick prayer and said we could all be seated. It was nothing like the prayers that they say in church or like the ones big mama prays but I was still glad that we could pray. I couldn't wait to go home and tell big mama she would be glad to hear it. Big mama always said that God is everywhere, and you should be able to pray to him anywhere and she was right. Even in school they let God in. 1 loved Mrs. Walker a whole lot.

We finally got a chance to play with the toys and then we had to eat lunch. We went to another big room where there were thousands of other children, and I saw my friends. But they wouldn't let us sit together, because they were in another class. Then after lunch we went back to the classroom and got ready to go home. Mrs. Walker explained to us that we were to get back on the same bus we got off of this morning. Mine was the giraffe bus. She hugged each of us at the door and the other lady that looked like us led us back down the steps to the room where we sat this morning.

"All those on the giraffe bus line up, your bus is here." Announced the lady that led us from the classroom. I stood up and William and I moved to the door. "Don't push, be nice to your classmates. The bus won't leave without you." We climbed on and I wanted to sit beside James cause I wanted to know how his class was, but the lady that rode on the bus with us wanted boys to sit with boys and girls to sit with girls. I didn't want to sit beside the girl I sat beside this morning because she talked too much so I sat beside a new girl I had never seen.

"Hi, I'm Camilla Garnet." I said. "I'm Jubilee Barnes." She replied. "Is this your first time at school?" I asked. "Yeah, I'm in kindergarten." She replied. "I'm in school." I replied. "My teacher's name is Mrs. Walker. What is your teacher's name?" "Mrs. White" she said. "Oh! Is this the first time you ever rode the school bus?" I asked. "Yeah!" Came the reply. I heard the lady call my name and I said what my teacher said we needed to say when we heard our name called. "Here." Jubilee looked funny. I sounded like the girl that was riding beside me this morning. I thought about being quiet. We started to move, and we passed a whole lot of other buses. We rode a long, long time and I sat by the window, and I didn't see anything I knew. Finally, we came to some familiar area.

Jubilee began to cry. "What's the matter?" I asked, "we are going to be home soon? Look, we are turning into the old school playground. I saw my momma. Do you see yours?"

She looked out the window and said, "Zebra." "What?" I asked. "Zebra, I was supposed to be on the Zebra bus." She cried. The bus stopped and the lady got off and helped everyone off. Jubilee was still crying. The lady asked her what the matter was as I stood behind her. Between her hissing sounds and choking noises she finally said she was on the wrong bus. By now my momma was up to the door waiting for me. "What seems to be the problem?" She asked the lady. "This child got on the wrong bus, and we can't take her back to the school because by the time we get there everyone will be gone." The lady said. "Well, come on here, baby sister!" That was all my mother had to say. "But momma, she is my friend. I don't want to leave her! Big mama says, that if you see somebody in need help them." It must have softened my momma's heart because she asked, "Baby what is your name?" "Jubilee Barnes." She replied. "Jubilee Barnes are you, Samuel Barnes daughter?" she asked. "Yes, Mam." she said choking back tears. "I'll take her with me," my momma said, "I know her parents and her father doesn't work too far from here. My name is Emma Mae Garnet, and I will make sure she gets home safely."

Quickly, I hugged my momma and grabbed Jubilee's hand. "You are just like Clemmy, if she saw a stray cat she would stop to help." My mother said. I smiled because I wanted to be like my big mama, she loved everybody, and she loved me the most. I didn't care if anyone thought I was like her because to me she was good all the time and she would never tell me anything wrong. I heard my mother say something about my clothes, but I was in a hurry to get to big mama.

We skipped to my house ahead of momma and I burst through the door to find big mama. I didn't have to look far, she was sitting by the window looking out. "I was waiting to see you get off the bus. How was your first day?" She asked as she hugged me. "It was great. Look, I have a friend. She got on the wrong bus and momma said she would make sure she got home safely." I told her. "She did?" Big mama said with surprise. My mother walked into the room. "Yeah, she twisted my arm. She is so much like you always going to get her point across. Let them stay here with you while I go next door and call her father. You girls play nicely together while I'm gone." Momma said. I didn't want to play, I wanted to talk to big mama and she knew it.

So big mama asked my friend what her name was. "Jubilee Barnes" she said. "Are you Samuel Barnes' daughter?" she asked. "Yes Mam," she replied. "Well, I'll be darn. Well Jubilee, you are a guest in our home and baby sister will let you share her toys. Won't you baby?" She asked me. "I sure will! I said but my name is Camilla Garnet." "I know that she said. You are named after me. My name is Camilla Hairston. Don't tell me you didn't know that?" She said with a puzzled look on her face. "I didn't want to disappoint her, so I changed the subject. "Little man's name is William Mason." "Okay! That's nice," she said, "now get some of your toys and you girls play right here on the floor." She left the room to go to the kitchen. Ladybug came downstairs from her nap and ran to me. "I missed you so much today!" I said giving her a big hug. "I missed you too. Can I go with you tomorrow? I don't want to stay here with momma and big mama they don't play with me, and they make me watch TV all day." Big mama returned to the room and momma was at the front door.

Well, I called her father at the bus station, and he will come and get her once he lets his wife know that she is safe." Sighed Momma. "Good!" big mama sighed in relief also. "Well in the meantime do you ladies want something to eat?" Momma asked. "We ate at school!" We replied together and then sniggled. "Well now would be a good time for a nap." My momma said. "Oh, Momma please! I have guests, can't I just play in the front yard?" "Okay but play nicely and don't leave the front yard." She said as she left the room towards the kitchen, I heard her say something about clothes again, but I didn't hear exactly what she said.

Jubilee and I head out the front door to the front yard. I was asking Jubilee about her father. She told me she had two parents, a mother and a father. She said her father had a job and so did her mother. I was really interested in finding out what a father did because I didn't have one. I had a mother (Emma Mae) A grandmother (Grandma Levy) Grandma Levy's mother (Sallie Lou) and Sallie Lou's mother.

(Big mama) my best mother. We didn't have any fathers in our family. Only mothers.

The front yard was small. The only thing to do in the front yard was to run up and down the hill, climb the shoemaker tree and act like we were riding a horse. But I had better not complain because I knew my mother if she said front yard, it was front yard or bed. Out the front door we went, me, Jubilee, Ladybug. I explained to Jubilee that there was not much to do but we could climb the shoemaker tree. Just then the door flew open. "Camilla Garnet" my mother screamed, "I thought I told you to change your school clothes." "I didn't hear you." I replied. "That's because you probably need your ears cleaned, or you were too busy trying to get home and out to play. Get upstairs and change your clothes. Jubilee, I don't think your mother would appreciate you messing up your clothes either, go upstairs with Camilla and she will give you something to put on."

We both went up the steps and I wondered why my mother was now calling me Camilla. I wondered what part big mama played in that name change. I didn't have many clothes and the stuff I did have, it was sometimes holey. That's what my mother called old clothes. Big mama would joke and say you got to be holy cause your clothes is. I found the best outfit I had and gave it to Jubilee, and I put on my favorite holey outfit. We laughed and giggled about the fit. It was just her size. And she liked it.

It was fun to have a girlfriend to share your clothes with. I would watch my older sister Tyra, she and her girlfriends shared their clothes and they had so much fun they were always giggling. I felt like a big girl. I pulled the hanger off the door and hung my dress on it and Jubilee threw hers across my bed. Rushing back downstairs and out the front door. I came to the front porch to find Ladybug in my big mama's arms, and she was telling her a story. I kind of got mad. But I remembered what big mama said to me one time. She said there is enough love to go around the world if you are not selfish with it.

So I turned to my new friend and said, "let's go ride the shoemaker tree." "Why you call it a shoemaker tree?" She asked. "That's because I stopped to think how should I explain it. I don't know but my big mama said that it is tuff as shoe leather to cut down, it has grown so much she can't shoo the birds out the top no more." That's the best I could explain it didn't matter she wanted to ride anyway. We rode for a long time.

Then Jubilee saw her mother and she ran down the hill. Her father was right behind her. They were coming up the back yard and she started out the front yard to the side of the house. "Jubilee, no! My mother said stay in the front she means stay in the front. I'll get in trouble if we leave the front yard." I explained. "Okay" she said. She was so nice she didn't want me to get in trouble, so we waited.

Her mother came to the front, and she ran to her. Jubilee's mother never spoke to my mother. Jubilee's father was thanking my mother on the side porch. Then I heard Jubilee's mother say, "You are so stupid! You couldn't even remember Zebra. How could you get up on the wrong bus? Why you got on them rags? Where's your clothes?" "They are upstairs." Jubilee said. "Go get your clothes and take them rags off and hurry up." Jubilee's mother said angrily. Jubilee's father and my mother were laughing, and he couldn't stop thanking her enough. Big mama was still sitting with Ladybug on the swing. Jubilee's mother said, "Thank you for keeping my child, Rev. Hairston." "I didn't keep her, Emma Mae did if you want to thank somebody thank the one who did it." Big mama told Jubilee's mom. "And just for the record children aren't stupid. She is just a tiny tot that made a mistake. You can't fault her for being confused, it's the first day of school. A grownup didn't check to make sure that she was where she should have been. But she isn't stupid, and I suggest you remove that word from your vocabulary when you speak to her again and especially while you are in my presence." Jubilee's mom started to look right funny and Jubilee came back dressed in her clothes. Jubilee's mother grabbed her hand and started out the front yard down the side steps. She called for her husband, and I heard him say, thank you again, to my mother and he jogged quickly to catch up with his wife, who appeared to be dragging Jubilee as she rushed to keep up. My mother came around the house from the side porch.

"Let's get ready for dinner, the other children will be here soon." Big mama said. "Did I hear that woman call my child's clothes rags?

The ungrateful" My mama said angrily "Hold it right there!" Big mama said. "You ain't do nothing wrong. You did it for your daughter and for the child. It doesn't even matter if you get no appreciation. It would have been the right thing for her to do but since she didn't. Just remember it's what's in your heart that matters to God and He would be proud of you. Cause I am. You didn't let your feelings for that woman stop you from helping her child." Big mama hugged my mother, and we all went in the house.

I was kind of mad cause I gave Jubilee my best outfit and I took the holey one for myself. I was doing just what big mama always said give your best. I guess my best wasn't good enough and I just hoped God would send me some more of those good clothes like I had this morning. I would take good care of them, and I wouldn't let them get to be rags.

Dinnertime came and went quickly, and I only had a short time with my big mama. So we headed for the front porch swing. "Big mama today in school I held the flag, and we said the salute to the flag. Then guess what we did?" Before she could answer I said, "we prayed. Mrs. Walker said I didn't have to get on my knees, in school we just stand quietly by our seats, and she prays. She didn't pray nothing like you or the preacher she was short and quiet. I played with toys, and we ate lunch in a big room where we had to stand in line with trays as the people behind the counter smiled and gave us all we could eat. Big mama most of them didn't look like me. I think they were white, but they were nice. Even the children were nice. It was a great day." I said with excitement. "I'm glad you enjoyed it." Big mama said sounding distant.

"Big Mama, why did Jubilee's mother call you Rev. Hairston? Is that your nickname?" "No baby girl, "Clemmy" is my nickname, and "Big Mama" is my nickname, but my real name is the same as yours, Camilla. The only difference is that you are a Garnet, and I am a Hairston because I got married. Rev. Hairston is my title. I preach and when you are a preacher, you are called "Reverend." she explained. "I never hear nor seen you preach before." I said. "That's because I'm old now. But trust me when it was my season, I taught the Bible, and I could give you the word. Now I just preach around the house let your mother tell it." Smiling she said "You had better get used to that title. You going to be wearing it someday cause you got a calling' on your life too." "Calling, what does that mean?" I asked. "Well child you will understand it better by and by!" she said.

One day I came home, and the old school yard was full of people going in and out of the old school carrying boxes and other stuff. I saw my oldest brother, Vandy and Mr. ATF. They were carrying boxes and talking. I got off the bus and big mama came to meet me. "Where is momma?" I asked. "She had to go to the doctor." She replied. "Is she all right?" I asked. "Yes, she just had to have a checkup she'll be just fine." She replied.

"Well, what's happening?" I asked. "They officially closed Jones Street School it is no more," she said sadly. "They are cleaning it out and Vandie is helping. Come on let's get out of the way so the men can finish." "Little Clemmy! Mr. ATF said. I have some things for you. I will send them home by your brother." "Thank you and God bless you." I replied. "I can tell you are raising her right, Rev. Hairston. She certainly is polite and cute as a button." He said to big mama. "Thank you and God bless!" Said my big mama as she held my hand, and we walked slowly towards home.

"Why are they closing the school, where are the big kids going to go to school?" I curiously asked. "That school is not for the bigger children, that school was where you would be going when you got to first grade next year. Come let's sit over here, I will explain it the best I can. You see since Dr. Martin Luther King Jr. started this great movement in our country to get us all to come together regardless of race. You remember seeing him on television, don't you?" She asked to make sure I knew whom she was referring to. "Yes, Ma'am and they have him on the fans at church too. Remember what the preacher said, if you get hot and before you blow your temper use the Rev. Dr. Martin Luther King Jr. fan to cool off and remember what he wants us to stand for!" I said in my low imitating voice. Laughing slightly, she said, "I can count on you to remember even the smallest of thin things. So that is why I share so much with you so someday you will live it.

Anyway, a lot of people are pushing to have both Negroes, that's us, and white people, that's people like your teacher and the bus driver to come together and live better lives. School is where children go to learn and get a good education so that when they grow up, they can become teachers and inventors and whatever they choose to be. In order to get a good education, you have to have good schools. Not every school has the same materials and tools to help you get a good education. The majority of people think that if they put together the schools and spend the money in the best ways the children like you can get the very best education they can get. It means that some of us have to make sacrifices, that means you have further to go to school and get up earlier, but I believe it will be worth it. Now some people like your mother, are against the move but she has a right to her opinion and so does everyone involve. Not everyone is ever going to see eye to eye on everything. People are always going to have a right to their own opinion, and you must respect that just like they must respect yours.

The Bible will tell us to try and live peacefully with all men aspiring to live a quiet life working with your own hands and minding your own business. Do that and you will be all right! I know you listen to my stories, and you ask a lot of questions, but I don't want you to get any wrong ideas. I know I have told you some stories about slavery times. You probably remember what I had to do when I was young and how some white folks treated me mean, but bad people are in every race and in every color. It doesn't mean that every white person you meet hates Negroes, nor does it mean that every Negro hates white people. Prejudice is wrong to dislike a person because of their skin color is what Martin Luther King Jr. is willing to give his life for. To change how people live and so that all men can one day live peaceably.

We all need to check our hearts and know that if we hate just because someone is different, we are prejudice. Love is the only thing that crosses color lines and brings everybody together on one accord. God is love and He wants us to love like him. I want you to remember this golden rule. Do unto others, as you would have them do unto you. In other words, treat people the way you want to be treated. Now you might not understand everything I am trying to teach you but if you put on your record player and remember these things, you will understand it better by and by."

I had a great deal to think about and I knew she was right. I had a good teacher, and she was white. I liked my classmates and some of them were white. All of them were good people so I guess I wasn't prejudice, and neither were they. So I didn't mind getting up early and going to school with different people, I just wanted to go to school.

I was staring down the schoolyard and I saw a figure coming up the old school yard. I couldn't tell who it was. Big mama said it was my mother. I couldn't see her until she was right in my face. I hear another voice call my name and it was my sister Ladybug right behind her. I hadn't seen her at all. I was just glad to see them. I hugged Ladybug and momma, and we all went into the house.

Later on, my brother, Vandy, came in the house carrying a box full of toys. "These are compliments, of old Jones Street School by way of Mr. ATF. He thought about you and picked you out some of the best learning materials the old school had to offer." He chuckled as he imitated Mr. ATF. As he placed the box on the living room floor, I saw some of the same toys I had in my school. I quickly started to explain each one to my sister Ladybug. Big mama had pulled her rocking chair from the corner to the middle of the room. "What have you got there; would you like to share with me too?" She asked. I started to explain each toy. When I got to the book with words and pictures, I pulled it close so that I could see the pictures and make up a story. All of a sudden, my head began to hurt really badly, it had happened to me several times in school before, but it really hurt bad now. I told big mama that it happens every time I look at letters. She motioned to me to come to her, and she rubbed it and kissed my forehead, and I felt better and went back to sit on the floor with my sister. It only stopped hurting for a little while and then it started again. I told her again and she repeated the process. Just about that time my mother called us in for dinner.

Dinner was really good today, momma and big mama did the combo cooking thing, they did that every once in a while, when there was more than one thing to cook. Today was brown beans, cornbread and fried chicken. We also had dessert, green tomato pie, it was big mama's best pie she had ever made. But she said I said that about every one of her pies. Because it was school time, I didn't have a whole lot of time to be with my big mama and she said that on Friday's I could stay up late and talk to her while the others watched *Chiller*. She didn't believe in those scary movies, and she said it would make you have nightmares and I would choose to sit in her arms and be rocked over a movie any day of the week. She told better stories than anything on television any way. Besides, TV made my head hurt.

Chapter 5

Rock Of Ages Cleft For Me

Song of Solomon 2:14
O my dove, that art in the clefts of the rock, in the secret places
of the stairs, let me see thy countenance, let me hear thy voice;
for sweet is thy voice, and thy countenance is comely.

Tonight, big mama said that she didn't want me distracted so she said that we would go upstairs and sit by the potbelly stove rock and sing. She had a heavy voice, but she could sing and she knew the words to lots of songs. She said her favorite song was Rock of Ages Cleft for me and that was where she would rather be. I want to know what she meant so I asked her "Big mama what is a rock of Ages cleft for me?" "She said I knew you would ask, and I am glad you did, now listen. First let's change into your bed clothes and say your prayers just in case you fall to sleep on me." "I would never fall to sleep on you." I said with a smile. "Stranger things have happened." She said smiling back. So we changed our clothes, pulled up to the stove, put a cover over us and started to rock in the big rocking chair.

"The Rock of Ages is God. A cleft is just a tiny little hiding place like on the side of a mountain. When a person climbs up, they have a little small ledge they can hang on to rest when they get tired. It's just enough so that they can get their second wind and keep on moving. It's not a place that you can stretch out and go to sleep, it's just enough to let you balance yourself, pull yourself together and keep on climbing. You see this journey in life is almost like the rough side of the mountain. It has places on the mountain that if you put too much weight on it will break off and leave you dangling. There are places on the mountain that are so slippery that even with the best gloves and shoes on you could lose your grip and fall. There are even places on the mountain, that are so sharp, that they will stab you if you touch them. When you climb the mountain you have to be very careful, very prayerful, very skillful. It requires you to look places over. Move and test some spots so that you can be sure it will hold you and give you support. Even then it is not always an assurance that you won't be deceived, but if you let God direct you, and you obey where he tells you to step, then you can find a cleft every now and then. So you can rest and get yourself together so you can keep climbing."

"People are just like the spots on the mountain. Some will support you and others will stab you, but you don't know which ones are which until you test them. Some people will say that they are your friends but baby when you get between and rock and a hard place they will disappear, and you can't find them. That's when you have to trust God to get you to safety. He provides the cleft that you need just to rest and get yourself together so that you can climb even when you got to climb by yourself. Now don't misunderstand me, there are times when you have to just trust somebody and believe in them, even when you have some doubt. That's when you meditate on God and ask him to direct that person in his will so that they can support you and help you get up the mountain.

God can turn anybody's heart anyway he needs to make sure his children get where he needs them to go. He got all power, and He knows everything and He is everywhere so if the person isn't going to do you no good He will let you know before the journey, during the journey or after you arrive. You got to listen out for God's voice so that you don't miss something along the way." "How does God speak to us?" I interrupted. "God speaks soft and sweetly. He got a still quiet voice that comes from inside you. It's like when you know something is wrong and you hear a voice saying go ahead and do it anyway. That isn't God. He would never tell you to do something wrong. If you know something is right and you just can't seem to do it and you hear a voice saying go ahead then you know it is God. But if you are not sure if it is right or if it is wrong or if you should do it then you listen carefully to hear his voice. Nine times out of ten, if you are concentrating on something, and need some help somebody might come along and confirm the right thing or show you the wrong thing. If you pay attention, then you will have your answer." "I don't understand" I said. "Well, you will understand it better by and by." She said.

"Well baby it looks like **Chiller** is over and it is time for bed, here comes everybody. Well tomorrow is Saturday. There are a lot of chores that need to be done so you get your rest good so that when I wake you in the morning you won't be acting grumpy like no knot on a log." Big mama said sweetly. "Okay I love you." I said. "I love you too baby girl" she replied as she kissed me on the forehead and hugged my neck. She hugged, kissed and told Ladybug she loved her too, but she was almost sleep and didn't say anything back.

I sleep so well. I even dreamed about climbing a mountain and in my dream, I saw big mama standing at the top of the mountain picking fruits from a tree, cheering me on and encouraging my steps. She just keep saying don't look back don't look back. I would reach out for a piece of rock, and I cut my hand, and I heard a voice behind me laughing. But I would not look back. I would reach for another and as soon as I got hold to it, I slipped and almost fell. I heard a voice behind me laughing but I would not look back. My hand was bleeding, and my knees were trembling, and I heard big mama say look for the cleft. I saw the cleft, I pulled up on it, got myself together and suddenly fear gripped me and I couldn't move. Just as I started to reach for the next level on the mountain, I heard a voice say. "What is the use? You are a failure and you ain't going to be no good for nothing. It sounded like a voice I knew. But big mama cried out, don't look back! So, I prayed God help me and before I knew it. I woke up.

I looked for big mama and she was nowhere to be found. I ran to the bathroom and washed up. I ran back to my room and put my clothes on quick as lightning. I needed to find big mama. I ran down the steps jumping down the last four. I peeked in the living room she was not in there. I ran to the kitchen; she was not in there. The washing machine was in the middle of the floor and the tub was up so I said to myself she was washing and she was outside. So I ran out the side door and down the steps to the yard. No one was there. A basket of clothes was sitting in the yard and the lines were full. I began to cry because I thought something had happened to my big mama. I walked back up the steps and I heard voices coming from the front yard. There sat my mother and big mama in the swing laughing and swinging. I ran to big mama, practically ignoring my mother. "Good morning baby" Big mama she said sweetly. "Is your sister awake?" my mother asked. Suddenly I couldn't answer, it was the voice I had heard in my dream that said I was going to fail. I was scared to death. I started to shake. My mother said, "Don't just stand there acting like a knot on a log I asked you if your sister was awake?" "Emma Mae, can't you see something is troubling the child." Big mama gently said. "I'll go see for myself." Momma said leaving the porch.

"Come here!" she said as she lifted me to her side.

"What's wrong did you have a bad dream?" She wiped the tears from my eyes and kissed my forehead. I didn't want to talk because I couldn't believe my dream and I didn't want it to come true and some parts of me did. So, I nodded my head up and down and then said, "Momma said that if you don't want a dream to come true eat breakfast before you tell it." I said as seriously as I could. "Oh, that is just some old wife's tale ain't no truth to that but come on it is time for breakfast it's just a little after 8:00 so cereal is in order. Go in the living room and watch TV until I fix you a bowl of cereal."

I was obedient and I went to watch TV. When big mama had come in with my bowl of cereal, she said put up the TV tray and said sit in that chair pointing to one in the corner close to the window. I was rubbing my eyes and my head was hurting. I told her that every time I looked at TV my eyes and head hurt. She left the room headed for the kitchen and I followed her. I wanted to tell her about my dream. She finished putting the milk on another bowl of cereal and handed me one of the bowls. I took a spoonful of cereal and gulped it down just in case there was some truth to what mama said, even though I believed big mama.

I told her how I was climbing the mountain and how she was on the top telling me to not look back. And how I had heard a voice telling me that I was no good and a failure. She and I walked back to the living room and sat down to eat our cereal. She listened to me and when I finished, she said, "I ain't no Daniel. He was the one in the Bible that interpreted dreams I can't say I can do that, but I will say this. That there are dream killers and there are dream stealers and there are dream fulfillers. You can't always tell who it is, for you and you won't always know what to do unless you guard your dreams and keep your eyes open. Always watch and pray and God will tell you what to do. I was truly confused now. How was I going to sleep with my eyes open? I was about to ask her when my mother came down the steps with my sister.

Big mama said, "Emma Mae, you need to get Camilla's eyes checked, she's been having a lot of headaches lately, and she's been rubbing her eyes a lot too." "Okay I will." she said as she rushed to the kitchen to fix Ladybug a bowl of cereal. All day long my head hurt until finally I couldn't help it no more. I told big mama I needed to see the doctor. She felt my forehead with the back of her hand and told me to stick out my tongue. She looked in my mouth and then in my eyes. She said you need glasses. I didn't know how she arrived at that conclusion what did feeling my head, sticking out my tongue and looking in my eyes have to do with needing glasses? I didn't understand it then, but I knew that I would understand it better by and by.

CHAPTER 6

There's A Preacher In The House

Romans 10:14
How then shall they call on him in whom they have not believed? And how shall they believe in him of whom they have not heard? And how shall they hear without a preacher?

Time seemed to be moving very fast I couldn't tell one day from the next and school was in one minute and out the next. I looked forward to going to church every Sunday and I wanted to hurry up and grow so that I could go to the Sunday school class for the big children. But it really didn't matter that much as long as I had a seat beside big mama during the service it was all right with me. This particular Sunday the preacher was in the hospital, sick, and every member of the church was there. We gathered around the altar and prayed he would get well. The deacon in the church read the morning scripture and the choir sang. Big mama had told me to stand beside mother Collie and be on my best behavior. She disappeared in the back. We had just finished praying when she came out in a robe one like the preacher wears. The deacon that gave the morning scripture said to everyone. "There is a preacher in the house. God would not leave us without a word, and He always has a ram in the bush. Stand and receive Rev. Camilla Hairston." I was already standing and so were most of the other people.

But somehow, I could not close my mouth. I was surprised because big mama said she was too old. She said everyone could take their seats.

We all sat down then she said "Giving honor to God who is the author and finisher of my faith and to all the saints that have come into the house of the Lord to praise him one more time. To all the visitors and friends and to my family that have come to support me as I lift up the name of Jesus." I started to look around and I didn't see any of her family in the church but me. She started to preach on faith. She said "Faith is the substance of things hoped for, the evidence of things not seen. Faith is something that you don't see but it works in you. If you trust God with everything you have and believe that he will do it in His time and in His assigned season you would be walking by faith and not by sight." She preached a long time, and I tried to meditate on her every word because if I trusted her as my big mama to tell me the truth, I surely trusted her as my preacher to teach me the truth.

We walked home and I asked big mama why did you say thank you to the family that had come when there was nobody from our family there. She said that anyone that belongs to the family of God belongs to her family.

She told me a story about when Jesus was teaching in the temple, and his mother and brothers came to find him. The disciples said that they were looking for him and Jesus asked the question, who is my brother and who is my mother? It wasn't because He had amnesia, and it wasn't because He didn't love them. He asked so that they might understand that whoever does the will of God is considered to be your brother and your mother in the house of believers. Big mama said that even if my own mother, brothers or sisters forgot about me, I would always have a family in the church where love has no limits. It had to be a church though where people loved and cared for each other and lived liked Jesus or it was counterfeit like a three-dollar bill. She made me promise never to forget that important piece.

When we finally got home and all sat down to dinner, I couldn't wait to tell everybody about big mama preaching. Nobody looked as excited as I was, but I keep on talking until my little brother told me I sounded like a preacher long winded and never knowing how to close my sermon. Nobody thought it was funny, and I think my mother was embarrassed because she started to turn red.

She was the first one to speak after that because big mama started to get up from the table. "Clemmy," she said, "Is Pastor Blaine out of the hospital yet." "No, he ain't any better yet and we don't know when he will return. If you will excuse me, I have to get ready for next Sunday." "Are you preaching next Sunday?" My mother questioned me. "I might." she replied.

As she left the kitchen, I saw tears in my mother's eyes and then she said to my little knuckle-headed brother that he needed to apologize to me and to big mama. He kept eating and said he would. He never said anything to me, and I never saw him go upstairs to big mama, but I did. When dinner was over, my mother shot out the door giving directions and chore duties and I went upstairs to my big mama. She was lying before the Lord and speaking in tongue. So, I eased in the room closed the door and knelt quietly beside her.

For some reason, school was boring all week long. I was not interested in doing anything. My head hurt all the time, and I couldn't read like the other children so in reading circle I would cry so I didn't have too. My teacher sent a note home to my mother and my mother was angry with me, but she didn't say why. I told big mama all about it and when she got my mother to herself, I was listening through the floor, and I heard everything.

Mrs. Walker who was now my first-grade teacher and had had me in her class for two years thought that I needed glasses. She had told my mother that last year. My mother told her we couldn't afford them, and she had found a Kwanza Club that would buy them for me. All my mother had to do was to take me to the white doctor. Big mama wanted to know why she wouldn't do it, and my mother said we had good doctors right down the street that we didn't need to go to no white neighborhood to see no white doctors for nobody's charity. Big mama said she was prejudice. My mother said that she would take care of it when she got her a job and had her own money and big mama said I could be blind before that happened. "Well, so be it," my mother said "but I'm not going to the white man's world as long as they hate us. I hate them." I had eased dropped on something that would hurt my feelings, shake my foundation and I could not talk about it because I wasn't supposed to hear it.

Sunday couldn't come fast enough for me because 1 needed to ask God to let me keep seeing and hurry up and give my mother the money to get my glasses cause she didn't have no job, and I didn't want to go blind.

Sunday was a marvelous day. The sun was shining bright and the sky as clear as crystal. Big mama woke me early before the sun rose and asked me to intercede in prayer for her. That meant that she and I would go to our secret closet, and I would pray, and she would pray and I would pray some more. It really meant that we went downstairs by the couch and knelt on the floor by the potbelly stove and prayed before anybody realized we were missing and got up to look for us. I loved to pray with her. She said we tag teamed the devil and we already had the victory. He just wouldn't submit. Big mama always made me feel so special. She told me that I prayed from my heart and that I must have been filled with the Holy Ghost early because I always knew what to say. I wasn't afraid of the Holy Ghost because she told me about Him too. She said he was a comforter, and he would teach me just like my teacher when I listened to the still small voice inside me. So I was not afraid of this ghost, he was like "Casper" the friendly ghost.

We got off our knees and went into the kitchen to get breakfast and Rufus the rat was in the kitchen scratching in the cabinet. I was afraid of him. Big mama stomped her feet and proceeded to put us some breakfast together. I hung close to her side. She went in the refrigerator and pulled out fatback, eggs and pancake mix. We keep it in there so Rufus wouldn't get any fatter. No sooner had she pulled out the skillet did Rufus jump from behind the refrigerator and run behind the sink. I screamed and woke the whole house up.

Everybody came running down the steps. Vandy made it to the kitchen first. "Rufus the rat was in here" I shouted. "Well, we can't seem to kill him for nothing in this world. Well, he'll live to see another day." Vandy said. Vandy always protected us. He was the man of the house, and he set the rattraps, fixed the fires and always did nice things for us and he loved Big Mama. I always caught him sneaking a kiss and bringing her flowers. "It's Sunday and were getting ready for church." Big mama said with a grin on her face. "Everybody that's going better get ready." Everybody left the kitchen and went to the living room to sit down. Big mama cooked and she and I finished eating quickly and returned upstairs to get ready for church. When we returned, we were ready for church and so we said our good-byes and started walking.

It was a lovely day, and we saw so many people up and on the street early this particular morning. Big mama seemed to know them all. As she spoke, she invited all of them to church and almost all of them said they would come. There was this drunken man that she called Mr. Bo Skeets, and he was so polite she invited him too. He said he would come too. I smiled because I knew they were all lying, she asked them to come every time she saw them, and they never showed up.

We were the first two at the church but not far behind us was the deacon and he had the key. He let us in, and he started to open windows and straighten chairs as he sang. "What a friend we have in Jesus." I joined in because that was one of my favorite songs and I knew the words. Big mama went to the altar and knelt in prayer. I helped him straighten up and pass out the hymnal and fans to each row of chairs. It wasn't long before all the regular members started to come in one after the other and each one joined in the song we were singing at the time. When it was time for service and we all gathered around the altar and prayed for Pastor Blaine, loved ones and sinners.

Big mama had slipped away and returned in the same robe she had on last Sunday. She looked different though this Sunday. She looked like I don't know she looked different. She came to the podium. The deacon announced her, he said, "Please stand for the speaker with a word from God for this house Reverend Camilla Hairston." She said the same thing she said last week. First giving honor to God, the author and finisher of my faith and to the saints and to my family. I knew what she meant about family, so I didn't need to look around no more because nobody would be there in our family but me. But she looked like she was going to cry so I had to just take a peek back there. I looked around and therein the back of the room I saw my mother, my sisters, my brothers, my grandmother and some other people I knew belonged in my family, but I couldn't remember their names. I wanted to cry because I remember hearing big mama pray to God asking him to let them come to church as a family just one time before she died. Then I got scared. I don't know why I got scared but I just felt scared.

Reverend Hairston preached love your neighbor as yourself. She said you had to love yourself before you knew how to love your neighbor. If you didn't care about yourself, how could you care about anybody else? But the first love was to love God who created you and to love Jesus who showed us the greatest love by laying down his life for us. She said you spell JOY, Jesus first, yourself last and others in between but you had to know who you were in Christ first to appreciate real L.O.V.E. She preached so hard and so fast that I was afraid she was going to get sick and then she called for all of those who wanted to have Christ in their lives to come to Jesus. The saints were praying, and I was watching. I was praying but I was watching too. I looked up and Mr. Bo Skeets was standing at the altar. He had come to church drunk, smelling like he had just drank all the liquor at the boot-leggers house and he was dirty.

He said, "I have been wanting for a long time to come through that door and give my life to Christ, but I didn't know how you felt about me. I am an alcoholic. Today when you asked me to come there was a different sound in your voice and I heard a still small voice saying it was time. You have always invited me and you have always shown your care in giving me something to eat, a warm blanket, or just a smile of encouragement. Please neighbor pray with me." He started to cry, and all the saints gathered around and prayed. The elders and big mama laid hands on him, and he went to his knees. They prayed and he stretched out on the floor. One of the deaconesses got the oil and boy he was really in God's hands then. They prayed, oiled, and spoke in tongue and hit him and he lay stretched out cold on the floor. I thought he was dead from all the people hitting him. He could not have been though cause too many of the saints were shouting and praying for him to be dead and nobody knew it. Finally, he got up. I had worked my way close to big mama and guess what he didn't even smell any more. He looked different and he did not say a word, he just got on his knees and cried.

After service was over, we all walked home together. The grown-ups walked behind and the children, my sisters and my cousins walked together. When we got home there was so much food. My cousins and aunts had made some food and brought it up from the patch. They lived in another part of the state, and we called it the patch. I don't know why, we just did. I wanted to know how everybody knew big mama was going to preach. Momma and my aunts were preparing the table I went upstairs to change my clothes.

I grabbed my T-shirt from off the bed and noticed that big mama was in the room with a pillow on the floor on her knees beside the bed. She was crying and praying and crying. I slipped over beside her, got on my knees, and knelt quietly. When she finished, I took my T-shirt and wiped her eyes. "Why are you crying?" I asked. "I am full," she said "I just had to thank God for answering my prayers. I knew he would do it because I have faith in him. However, it was just so much more than I had expected." She said still crying. "Well sometimes God surprises us. You always say that he will do exceedingly and abundantly more than we ask or expect." I said, "You are so right baby and don't you forget it. Now help me up so we can go eat." Big mama said, she was now smiling.

As she stood to her feet, it seemed to me, she had a glow. Her face was bright or was it my eyes playing tricks on me. Either way I knew she had been in the presence of God because I remember what she said about Moses that when he came down from seeing God, he was bright as a light. I think she really saw God. She rubbed my hand and waited for me to change my clothes.

Then she went to the bathroom, I was right behind her. She blew her nose, washed her face, and dried her hands then she turned to me and said, "Don't never let them see you cry when they can't understand your tears." I didn't quite understand what she meant. Just about that time I heard my mother calling my name. I said, "Here I am I'm coming now." So big mama and I walked down the steps. I wondered all through dinner what she meant, about not letting them see me cry. One time, she said it was all right to cry because it shows you have feelings, now she said don't cry. I couldn't wait to ask her but better yet, I guess I will understand it better by and by.

CHAPTER 7

Plant, Water And Watch It Grow

I Corinthians 3:6-8.
I planted Apollas watered, but God gave the increase.
7.So then neither he who plants is anything, nor he who waters,
but God who gives the increase. Now he who plants and he who
waters are one, and each one will receive his own reward
according to his labor.

Big mama was a gardener. Everyone in town said she had a green thumb. Every now and then when I held her hand, I would look for it, but I couldn't see it. It was a lovely spring day, and I had just got off the bus from school. I looked to see who was out there to meet me and I saw no one. So I headed up the old school yard home. When I reached my house, the yard was torn up and all I could see was black dirt. "Oh my goodness somebody done stole the grass!" I said to myself and then I sped inside to tell big mama. When I reached the door, through the screen I could see big mama standing in the kitchen with gloves on her hands and a big straw hat on her head. Out of breath I blurted, "Big mama somebody done stole the grass." She burst out laughing. "Come her child and give me my hug." She bent slightly to hug my neck and then explain. "I plowed up the yard to make a garden. She chuckled, "Would you like to help?" "Sure," I replied. "Well, change your school

clothes and be sure to put on some old clothes cause this is dirty work."
"Okay" I said as I bounced up the steps to my bedroom.

I changed quickly and came back to the kitchen. "Here!" She said handing me a bar of soap. "Rub your fingernails across it and make sure the soap gets under your nails. Then put on these gloves." She instructed and placed the gloves on the counter. "You don't want me to wash my hands first?" I said, thinking I had missed something. "No baby girl when we get through, we will wash our hands and you won't have any dirt under your nails." I did as she instructed as quickly as I could. I was excited and I didn't want her having to wait for me. Even if it took me until dinner she would wait because she said, "Patience was a virtue." Whatever that meant. Finishing up I turned to her and said, "All done." "Good, now help me with these trays. Be very careful going down the steps. Don't touch the plants until I tell you. Okay?" she said. "Okay" I replied.

She opened the screen door with her foot as she carried a tray in one hand and a jug of water in the other. I started to grab two trays, but she told me to just grab one that between the two of us, that would be all we would be able to plant today. She said making a good garden takes lots of time, work and patience. You had to plant the seed just right to get a good harvest. Carefully I carried my tray out the door and down the steps. Making sure I didn't touch the plants. When I reached the bottom big mama was just on the second step creeping down humming a hymn. I was excited and anxious to get started and big mama was walking as if she didn't have a care in the world and nowhere to be anytime soon.

"Go over there to the spot where they stole the grass." She teased. I walked over to the wide-open spot and stopped. "Big mama, there is a shovel and an axe out here on the ground, why?" I questioned. "Yeah, stop right there." She was moving a little quicker now. "Don't move baby and be quiet. Do you hear me?" She insisted. I shook my head up and down to acknowledge her. She put the tray and jug down almost dropping them. So, I lunged towards her and she shouted, "I said don't move!" I froze dead in my spot. She moved faster than I had ever seen her move. She trotted over to the axe, picked it up and then she came right next to me, walked a couple of steps, raised the axe over her head and struck the ground twice. "Got ya' Satan. I've been looking for you all day to peek your head up here so I could chop it off!" She sounded joyful and she sounded angry. But I was afraid to move because I knew how much she hated Satan. So if she was chopping up Satan I didn't want to see what he looked like when she finished. Still frozen into position, she announced that I could turn around now. I turned to see a green snake about as long as my arm wiggling on the ground. I started to scream. "Okay quiet down child, he's dead now, he can't hurt you." Immediately I stopped screaming, even though I saw it moving and wiggling on the ground. If big mama said he was dead, then he was dead. I believed her cause she would never tell me anything wrong.

"Now just stand still until I look over the rest of the yard. Satan might have some brothers and sisters out here." She said as she surveyed the ground with her eyes and eased over to the shovel and picked it up. Then she took her time and went over every inch of the yard. Finally, she was through. I keep silent the whole time she inspected. "Well, all's well that ends well. Here, hold the shovel." She said as she motioned me over to where the snake lay. "Put the shovel here, and we are going to get rid of Satan once and for all." I held the shovel trembling to think that Satan almost had me. I got away only because big mama would never let anybody, or nothing hurt her family. Smiling, I thought how brave she was and how she protects me. All I had to do was listen to her. I knew she was going to always tell me the right thing to do, and I could certainly trust her with my life. Big mama was my super woman.

Satan had stopped wiggling and once big mama raked him onto the shovel, she told me to carry him over to the cardboard box and dump him in. She told me to move quickly because we had plenty of work to do and Satan had already tried to slow us down. So, I moved quickly, dumped the snake, brought back the shovel and said, "Let's get to getting it. One snake doesn't stop no show." "Now that's what I like to hear. Get the trays and follow me."

I picked up mine and she picked up hers and the jug of water. We moved to the farthest part of the yard where she started to give instructions. "Now listen, this is my garden, and I want it done right. Most of the time when a person wants something done right, they do it themselves. But because I believe in you, and I know you will do it

right. I'm depending on you to listen and do what I say, okay!" "Okay"'
I replied.

"Now I forgot the hand shovel, I know it's around here
somewhere." She said. "What does it look like?" I asked. "It's a small
tool that looks like the big shovel. I know it's around here, I had it
this morning." She said still surveying the yard. "I saw it. It was over
by the cardboard box. I'll get it for you. I will be right back." I said as
I skipped over to the box. As I reached down for the shovel I peeked
in the box. Satan was moving. "He's alive!" I shouted, "Satan done
come back alive." "Come on here child and leave that snake alone he's
as good as dead but the sun ain't gone down yet, so he will move until
then." I ran back to her "What do you want me to do?" I asked. She
knelt down put one hand on the ground and then the other as she sat
down. "You see these rows; I made them for the plants. Each plant
needs a hole and some dirt to go around it. Make each hole about so
deep." She illustrated by doing one. "Then I take the plant out the tray
stick it in the hole and cover it around with dirt like so press down the
dirt just a little, so you don't smoother the root and then we water and
watch it grow." She smiled as she showed me every step of the way.
"That's sounds easy!" I said anxious to get started. "Well, it is a trick
to this. "The trick is to space each plant with enough room for it to
grow to its fullest potential. I believe I'm going to let you plant then I'll
water, and we will watch as God gives the increase." She said.

I moved over to the row next to big mama. I dug the first hole.
"How about this?" I said. It was too deep. So, I covered it with dirt
and started again. This time I only dug a little. "Not enough." She
said. I dug some more. "Too much." she said. I was getting a little
frustrated when I looked over at her row and she had already planted
three plants. "Big mama I don't think I'm ever going to get this right." I
said frustrated already. "Yes, you will but only if you don't ever give up.
It doesn't matter how many times you have to start over just finish what
you start and get it right." She encouraged. "Now let me let you in on a
secret. When you dig the hole put your finger in it if your whole hand
can go down in it. It is too big. If your finger can go down about two
inches or so it is just right." I listened and did what she said. "Perfect!"

came her response. "Now make me about a dozen of them perfect holes in one row going back and I'll give you the plants."

We worked as a team and before I knew it, we had my tray, and her tray planted. "That's enough for one day," she said. We had better go get cleaned up for dinner your mama and everybody will be here soon." No sooner than she had got the words out of her mouth, a cab pulled up the old school yard. "That's them now." she said. I headed for the cab. "Hey, where are you going?" she asked. "To meet mama." I replied. "And leave me sitting here on the ground." she asked. I looked over at her and she was smiling so I smiled back and asked, "Do you need help?" "Everybody needs some help every now and then." She said. As she stretched out her hand, I took hold of it and gently pulled as she moved to her knees and using her other hand stood up. By now the cab was parked in our back yard.

Mr. Nubby got out and came around the cab, opened the door for my mother. Ladybug busted out the cab's back door. "Hey, hold up young lady!" He said to ladybug. "Always let a man at least have a chance to open your door." "Okay!" she said running to give me a hug. "Where y'all been?" I asked, "To the grocery store, we got a whole lot of food too!" she said. I skipped over to the cab. "Who got all this food?" I asked. "Stop asking questions and carry them bags in the house," my mama said. Mr. Nubby handed me a bag. I carried the first bag in and rushed back out to get the rest. When I returned everyone was home. My sister, both brothers and my mother all had a bag, even Mr. Nubby. "That's the last one." He said. As I met him on the steps, that lead to the side porch. "I see you have been working in garden, do you have a green thumb?" He asked. "I don't know," I replied, "I haven't taken my gloves off yet." He laughed and walked down the steps chuckling all the way.

Back inside my sisters and brothers were putting up the food and big mama was at the sink. "Come on here, baby girl, and take them gloves off and wash your hands." She beaconed me. I walked over to the sink where she was standing. I was scared to take off my gloves because I didn't want to have a green thumb. The children at school had started to laugh at people who were different. Slowly I took off the first glove, no green thumb. Then I removed the second. "Ah!"

I sighed in relief. "What was that for?" Asked big mama. "Cause I thought I would have a green thumb when I took my gloves off!" I said. Everybody started to laugh. "I've heard it all," my brother Vandie said. A little embarrassed I said, "No you haven't. Big mama killed Satan out in the yard, and I threw him in the cardboard box." "What?" Vandie asked. "You heard me." I replied. Well, it must have gotten his attention because he headed for the door and as the screen door closed with a bang my mother said. "Now what did you tell him that for you know he has a fascination with snakes. "Well, I hope he doesn't bring it in the house!" said Tyra. Then we all laughed.

It seemed to rain every day for the next month or so. Every morning, I would have to get up and put on my yellow raincoat and goulashes and walk to the bus stop. It seemed to me that every child in my class had a school bag to put their things in. I had to hang up my raincoat and place my goulashes in the corner. By the time school was over each day, the sun was shining, and it was too hot to wear the raincoat so I had to carry it and my goulashes in my hand, which was quite awkward along with my homework. But somehow, I made it. When I got home one evening my mother wasn't there, but my big mama was and I told her how the other children had a school bag made of plastic and some had pictures. She said I don't know if I can buy you one like that, but I will see what I can do. She found a Piggly-Wiggly bag and gave me a big black crayon and told me to write my name on it. She told me if I want to draw a picture it would make it personal. She said it should work until she was able to get me another one. She said when I got to school, I could organize my things by folding them neatly and putting them in a bag then carrying them would be easy. Big mama always had a solution. I asked her where was momma and she said she had gotten a job. I was so proud of her I didn't think to ask her what kind I just knew she wanted to work, and she had been looking a long time.

Big mama had cooked, and dinner was soon to be served because all my sisters and brothers were coming in the house. They knew what time dinner was served and nobody was ever late. "I have to get some fresh onions out the garden," announced big mama "would you like to go with me?" "Sure!" I replied and down the side steps we went. I really had not notice just how big the garden had grown but standing in the yard next to green bean poles and the tomato vines and the cornstalks made me look short. It was the first time I had really noticed that the sticks had been placed next to each plant. "Big mama why come those sticks have, grown up on our plants?" I asked. "Oh, you silly child those sticks don't just grow they have to be placed there. You see the string? I come out here and work my garden. I put the sticks next to each plant to train them as to how they should grow. I put a string around them because if they get to heavy, they will lean to the side and not grow as straight and tall as they can. I come out and pull up the weeds so that they won't steal the good soil from the plant and stunt its growth. A garden is a lot of work, but it is rewarding when you can put food on your table and give some to others."

"Baby sister. You know you are God's little human garden. I'm like the stick I stand beside you and help you to grow straight. The string is like my rules they hold you in line and even if they seem too tight, they keep you in place and won't let you stray too far. The word of God weeds out the garden. It tells you what is good and what is bad and when God starts to work in your heart, He won't allow the weeds to choke out the good plant and steal the good soil so you can't grow. Sometimes he takes away people that don't mean you any good and sometimes he moves danger so you won't get hurt. But it always requires you to do your part to work at keeping your garden weed free and growing straight. Cause God knows how much rain you need and can take so that it doesn't ruin your roots, and he knows how much sunshine you need so that you don't get scorched or dry up at the roots. God is just amazing." She said now smiling from ear to ear. "You know I believe you will grow to be a great garden and produce good fruit. That's why I work so hard to show you that with faith in God and with believe in yourself you can do anything you want to do. Well, you might not understand it now but you will understand it by and by." "Well big mama, I know you are right!" I said. "But there is something I want to do, and I need your help?" Looking a little surprised she said, "What is it baby girl? You know if I can, I will do it." She said in her serious voice. "I want to plant my own garden and work it just like you. You think I can do that?" "I think you can do anything you put your

mind and your hands to; after all you got a whole lot of me in you."
She said with a little brag.

Grandma and Grandpa Newsome from next door were driving
up into their carport. Grandpa Newsome had built himself a shelter
for his car between our house and his and he was real proud of it. In
between his house and ours was a small strip of dirt with some logs
around it. As they got out of the car they were smiling and waving
at big mama and me. "Praise the Lord! Rev. Hairston." he said. "And
how are you today?" he asked me. We both replied together praise the
Lord. Grandpa Newsome asked me how I would like to make some
money by carrying his groceries in the house. I told him I would love
to, so I carried all the bags up the steps and onto his porch as quick as
a flash. When I finished, he, grandma Newsome and big mama were
talking, and talking, he stopped long enough to reach in his pocket
and pull out a quarter. I said "No, thank you. I carry a friend's bags
for free." Grandma and Grandpa both reach out to give me a hug.
Grandpa said to big mama, "she is quite a young lady." "That she is,"
big mama replied. "She wants to be a gardener too!" She said with a
laugh. "I suppose she will be a good one like you." Interjected, grandma
Newsome. "Well, there is never any time like the present to train her"
said grandpa Newsome. "I would love to see if she has a green thumb
like you Rev. Hairston. How bout I do a little planting in her life?
You see that little spot right there I was going to plant some flowers in
that spot, but I will let her plant herself a small garden if she wants to.
How does that sound to you baby sister?" He asked me. "I would be
honored." I said trying my best to sound grateful cause I really was, but
I didn't really know what to say, so I said what I heard my big mama say
when someone invited her to do something. "Well, it's settled you got
prime real estate for free. All I want in return is to taste some of Rev.
Hairston's cooking every now and then." "Well, I think we can handle
that." Replied big mama as they shook hands.

As they said their good-byes big mama was smiling and almost
looked like she wanted to cry. "What's wrong?" I asked. "Oh ain't
nothing wrong. I am just overwhelmed. I thought about that space
when you asked me but I would never image that God would make a
way that fast." She shook her head in her rejoicing manner. I almost

knew what she meant, because Grandpa Newsome was always so particular about everything around his house and our neighborhood and not that he wasn't friendly. He just seemed so, I can't explain. He was a good man. Even though my big mama seemed surprised, I know in my heart she knew that God's favor was on her life. All she had to do was speak the word, and God would change the heart of a king to make sure her desires came true. Big mama was truly God's child.

I asked her why she was so happy for me that she would sound as though she was rejoicing. She told me she was doing just that rejoicing. She said when God blesses someone else you need to rejoice because sometimes it is a blessing in disguise for you also or it means that yours is on the way. Either way never be stingy and jealous of what good things God does for someone else because whatever He did for one of His, He is capable of doing for the other that is what a good parent does for each of his children. He blesses them with what is good, necessary or needed at the appointed time.

After dinner that night, big mama went to the front porch and placed newspaper on the table. She brought out six small flowerpots and told me to get the hand shovel so that we could test the soil in the spot we were going to plant my garden. I asked if Ladybug could help if she wanted to and she nodded her head okay. I asked Ladybug to help me find the hand shovel and to dig up my garden. She was truly excited. We skipped down the steps to the coalhouse and looked just inside the door and picked up the hand shovel and started back. Then Ladybug asked me why were, cages behind the coal bin? I had never noticed them before, I started to wonder was I going blind because they were so big how could I have missed them? Back up the steps we went and into the front yard to find big mama waiting patiently for us.

Here girls take the shovel and dig up enough dirt to fill each one of these pots and bring them back. We both filled three a piece. I told my sister that I could divide, I had learned it in school, but really I counted one for you and one for me, until each of us had three apiece. Then I said six divided by two equal three. Boy was she ever proud to have such a smart sister.

After we brought the filled pots to big mama, she poured out our dirt on the paper and told us to take out all the little pebbles and rocks and put them into one of the empty pots. She had a hand full of brown beans (pintos) and she said we would be able to plant them once we made the dirt ready. "Brown beans, were going to plant brown beans?" Asked Ladybug. "Yes! We're going to plant brown beans but before we plant them, I want to tell you a story." Big mama said. I got so happy that I almost knocked all the dirt off the table. Big mama was going to tell me a story and Ladybug was going to hear it for herself. It was a moment I had wanted to share with her forever.

Big mama pulled up a chair and started. Well, let me begin by saying that in order for a seed to grow into a new plant it must first die in the ground. We sleep and rise day after day and then we notice that the plant has started to grow but we don't know how. Yet the plant grows and gets larger and larger until it bears food for us, and we harvest the fruits of our labor. We are only used of God to do the planting and sometimes the watering, but God gives the increase. We never know how much our little seeds will produce. It might seem to you, that they are small and unimportant but because God has the final say and he grants the seeds to the sower. (That's you and me). We can rest assured that it will always be more than we had expected or for that matter even deserve. I just want you girls to remember that if you plant bean seeds you will harvest beans, if you plant kindness, you will harvest kindness. A plant only produces what was planted and nothing different. So if you plant hatred you will get hatred in return. There is a scripture that says "God is not mocked whatever a man soweth that shall he also reap. "That means you reap what you sow. Say it with me "You reap what you sow." We repeated. "That means whatever you plant is what you get back." I said, "Keep picking the pebbles out to the soil, Ladybug, you can listen and work at the same time." Said big mama. "But I don't understand," said Ladybug. Simultaneously big mama and I both said, "You'll understand it better by and by."

CHAPTER 8

Tamara You Got To Deal With It!

2 Samuel 13:3
But Amnon had a friend; whose name was Jonadab, the son of Shimeah David's brother and Jonadab was a very subtle man.

I was getting older now and was being allowed to play outside more. I wasn't ever allowed to leave the yard unless I had an older sister or brother with me so today, I wanted to follow my knuckle headed brother. I heard at school that my brother was very mischievous and that he didn't always do the right things, but I knew right from wrong and I wasn't about to break no trust bonds with my mother and especially with my big mama. So I convinced my big mama to let me play with my brother. Big mama told him that he had to watch out for me and not to leave me by myself. He nodded okay and said, "Can I go now?"

"Just a minute!" Big mama said giving me my instructions. "I will let you go out and play against my better judgment, but I declare if you don't behave yourself, you can't do that no more you understand me baby sister." She looked serious and she also looked worried, so I promised. I told her that I would always make her proud and she would never have to worry about me doing nothing wrong, trust me! I often heard my big sister say that and she was always good and never got into any trouble. So I just mimicked her words but deep down I really meant them.

Mom had gotten a good job, and she was working dayshift and coming in late. Big mama was doing the cooking, cleaning and babysitting. Well just as soon as I left the porch my brother started to run, and I couldn't keep up with him so I started to cry. Big mama called me back and told me I just needed to stay with her. But I told her that if I ran fast, I could catch up with him. So that's just what I did I ran so fast that I surprised myself. I caught him and told him he had better not leave me again or he was going to have to explain his actions to big mama when he got home.

He laughed and told me that he had a secret and if I wanted to hear it I had to do what he said. "Well, what's in it for me? What do I care about your secrets? If it ain't a good secret, I'm going to tell on you so you better not be up to no good." I stood in his face with my hands on my hips to let him know I wasn't playing. "I knew I shouldn't have let you come with me. You are a party pooper and a snitch. He said. "Do you know what the streets do to snitches?" He was giving me the evil eye, so I backed up off him a little ways and said "No and I don't care. Do you know what big mama does to boys that don't do right?" I said. He stepped to me and pushed me then said "Go home before I punch you in the mouth you smart aleck. I'm going to play hide and seek and it's not for no snitch. So you had better run your narrow behind home."

Just about that time I spotted his friend the boy who couldn't hardly talk the one that my brother was supposed to be buddies with and the one I was scared of. "Hey Pooch!" Shouted my brother. "Ready, set let's go and get it." Pooch stuttered, he was much too old to be on the playground and every time one of the older people saw him out there with little children they would chase him off. People said he was short in the head and that trouble followed him like the devils hallow. I was scared of him cause no matter where he saw me, he would say things like IIII 'm gu nnna ggget soome of tatt pppp I couldn't ever understand what he was trying to say and most of the time before he was able to get his sentence out I was gone. Today he wasn't stuttering very much. "I got some new nickels and a bag of candy man do a good job and I will give you some." He told my brother.

I had no idea what job my brother had but I didn't like what I heard, it just didn't seem right. Pooch was a strange acting boy and he was bigger than my brother, and I heard he could fight too so I felt like he was making my brother work for him but I didn't know how. "You stay right here my brother told me. And wait for the other kids your age to come out and play as a matter of fact here comes some now." I looked and sure enough there were two girls that I went to school with coming up the playground. I got excited and ran to meet them then I stopped for some reason. When I turned around to tell my brother he was right. He and Pooch were gone. They just disappeared. I thought my eyes were playing tricks on me. So I looked behind the hedges and under the school steps but they weren't there. I called out for them, and no one answered.

By now, my friends had reached the playground, and we started to talk. They asked me how I was let out to play all by myself. They told me that we had to stay together because there were some boys that were hurting girls in the neighborhood, and they always carried a stick when they came out to play. I looked at the stick my friend Lisa had, it looked like the leg of a coffee table and the one Lynn had looked like a baseball bat. "Well, I need to find me a stick," I said. "You sure do!" They said. "How about we look up on the hill and pick you out one." Lisa said. "That would be great, but my brother told me I needed to stay here until he came back." I said. "It won't take but a minute!" They said convincing me that it was better to have a stick and not use it than to not have one and need it.

So up the hill we went on the side of the school and no stick. Around the corner we went and no stick "I will look over here" said Lisa, " and I will look over here," said Lynn "you keep going straight up the hill." Then just as I thought I had spotted a stick someone grabbed me and put his hand over my mouth. I couldn't see who it was, and I couldn't yell. I tried to kick and pull away, but they were stronger than I was. I could tell it was a boy because he was strong and had a boy's arm. He pushed me to the wall and started to pull my pants down. I started to cry and kick harder and then, I heard my friend Lynn scream. I saw

Lisa run towards where I heard the scream come from with her stick, but someone must have had Lynn because I heard her Lisa saying. "Let her go you nasty boy."

I kicked and scratched and tried to get loose finally I was able to bite the hand that held me, and he slapped me across the face hard and kept trying to put his hands on my privates because my pants were now down to my knees. I could finally see it was Pooch. He hit me again with his fist in the face and knocked me to the ground. I started to scream, and he grabbed my mouth with one hand and his privates with the other. He was now trying to lie on top of me as I struggled to get free, I hear someone running towards us. It was my friend Lisa, and she had her stick swinging, and she hit him in the head. She hit him as hard, I saw stars. He was now lying on the ground trying to cover up as she swung again and again. I was free now and she was running back up the side of the building swing the stick at the other guy. I could see Lynn, she was pulling up her panties.

So I touched my face and my nose was bleeding. I started to scream and tried to pull up my clothes so I could run too. I pulled up my clothes and ran toward my friends. As I got closer, I saw my brother running up into the woods and across the street. I looked back and Pooch was getting up off the ground running towards us. "Let's go!" Shouted Lynn. So we ran as fast as we could to the end of the schoolhouse. We must have been screaming all the way because before I knew what was happening "Mr. GI Joe" was up the hill and chasing Pooch. Grandpa Newsome was half up the hill reaching for us girls and big mama was standing in the backyard asking what was happening and were we all right.

Well, there was confusion everywhere. "Mr. GI Joe" had Pooch by the neck coming down the hill beside the school and grandpa Newsome was calling to Grandma Newsome to call the police. Big mama was just running to the end of the yard to meet me crying. I had never seen big mama cry in front of other people. I saw my brother Vandie running up the schoolyard and questioning everybody as to what was going on. Big mama grabbed me and rushed me into the house and started to place ice on my nose. Grandpa Newsome took my friends by the hand and led them behind big mama and me into our house. When we got inside Grandpa Newsome pointed to my pants and big mama began to scream and shout Jesus almost like she does in church but much more like she was in pain. My brother Vandie came busting though the door and asked me who did it. I told him Pooch and he flew out the door with Grandpa Newsome following him calling him, begging him not to do anything. There was confusion everywhere. My friends stood in the kitchen crying frantically, and then Grandma Newsome had made her way into the house to help us out. "Are you girls alright?" she asked. "I'm fine" I said clinging to big mama. "Are you all right, Rev. Hairston?" She asked big mama. "I'll be fine. Thanks for helping with other girls." She said kind of pushing them towards her. "Oh yeah!" She said examining them. Big mama took me to the big rocking chair in the living room and rocked me as she applied the ice to my nose. She rocked and prayed and prayed and rocked, she cried and prayed and rocked and cried.

It seemed like hours had passed and big mama was still rocking me. My mother came rushing through the door with her mother and her grandmother. Someone had called out the MBA's Mother's that Beat Your---. Grandma Levy lived in Wisconsin, and she only came to town twice a year, once in May, for Momma's birthday, she would stay two or three weeks, and then return again in September for her birthday and to get us ready for school. (She made us the greatest outfits and could sew as good as her mother.) That's why she lived in Wisconsin (she was a seamstress for the white people, and they paid her big money). So when she went on vacation she would come and stay all month long.

Today they came to go to war cause I had never hear such language. There was so much hollering and screaming and cursing that big mama put her hands over my ears. Momma just lay in the floor by the chair and told big mama to give me to her. Big mama still had not stopped crying but as my mother stood up, she handed me over to my mother and momma started to carry me towards the steps that lead upstairs.

Then the police came in the house. They told my mother that they had caught one of the boys that had hurt me, and he was in the ambulance. Then they put handcuffs on my brother Vandie and told my mother that they were sorry that they had to do this and they were sorry for what had happened to me but my brother had to go with them downtown. I looked and the policeman was crying. I told them my brother Vandie didn't hurt any of us girls and he told me that that was true, but he had taken matters into his own hands, and he had to face the consequences, they had no other choice. I had no idea what that meant.

There was another officer that was talking to my friends, and they told them it was my other brother that attacked Lynn. So now everybody was screaming again. My mother put me down and ran to the kitchen. She asked the girls how did they know it was my brother? Lina pointed to the picture on the wall straight ahead in the living room and said, "That was the boy that tried to hurt me." My mother couldn't believe it but I knew it was true I saw him run up into the woods.

The tall white police officer came over to talk to me, said he was so sorry for what had happened to me and to my friends. That he had two little girls and if someone harmed them, he believes he would have done what my brother Vandie did. The other white officer was talking to my mother saying, "Mrs. Garnet, I am so sorry for what I have to do to your sons, but we will straighten this whole matter out. When your youngest son comes in to tonight make sure you call us so we can come and talk to him." My mother covered her mouth and nodded her head as the tears streamed down her face. Big mama was still sitting in the chair staring into space. Momma crying, a police officer cuffing and carrying my good brother off to jail, Grandma Newsome hugging my friends, their mothers coming through the door crying, my sisters being lead out of the house headed to I don't know where by the MBA's lead lady Sallie Lou. What in the world was going on? I didn't care about me right then I couldn't understand why they took my good brother away. I went back over to where big mama was sitting and asked her why they took him he hadn't done anything. She said, "He was wrong he almost beat the life out of Pooch and that was wrong of him because he wanted to do it."

My mother's mother Grandma Levy was now all up in the house. She picked me up and headed up the stairs and big mama was on the move to follow. Momma was still trying to absorb what had happened and her grandmother Sallie Lou was protecting my bad brother's honor as she prepared to lead Ladybug and Tyra out the door and pass the police. What a mess! Up the stairs we went and into the bathroom with big mama rushing to climb the stairs in hot pursuit. Grandma Levy had me in her arms and I was now facing the mirror, I hadn't seen my face until now and I started to scream. It looked as though I had been hit in the face by the baseball bat. There was dried blood everywhere and my nose was as big as a baseball. "It's okay you will be all right." Grandma Levy said. "Here Clemmy, you wash her face while I take these clothes off! Here stand up straight child." Grandma Levy pulled my pants down and she started to scream and the words that came out of her mouth would have put a sailor to shame. "Oh! He is a dead man!" She said as thy mother and grandma Newsome rushed through the door. My mother fell to her knees in tears and grandma Newsome started to restrain grandma Levy as she tried to head for the bathroom door and big mama, well she just cried and cried.

There was lots of hugging and crying and then silence. It felt like forever and then my mother spoke and said, "How could this happen Clemmy what were you thinking letting my baby go out by herself?" Big mama started for the door with her hand over her mouth and tears still streaming down her cheeks. I started screaming, it's not her fault and clinging to her leg so she wouldn't leave me. Then everybody started to hug everybody again and cry over top of me. Grandma Levy picked me up in her arms and held me close to her big chest. It felt like it was raining on my head, from all the tears they shed that day. Finally, grandma Levy let go and placed me up on the commode top and started to wipe me up.

Grandma Levy wanted to know did the boy hurt me down in my private area. I noticed blood in my panties, and I started to tell them what had happened. I told them that when Pooch hit me in the nose and knocked me to the ground and tried to get on top with his private parts in his hand one of my friend's hit him in the head with a stick. I told them that my nose was bleeding so bad that it had dripped into my panties as I rushed to pull them up and started to run.

Well, it must have made things better because I heard a sigh of relief from my mother. Grandma Levy still wanted me to go to the hospital and Grandma Newsome was in agreement. So big mama left the bathroom and returned with me some good clothes and they dressed me, and Grandma Newsome went to get Grandpa Newsome to drive me to the hospital and to take mama to the jailhouse. Grandma Levy said she was going to wait for Mr. Knuckle Head to come home. Big mama grabbed her coat, walking stick and me, and we went to get in the car with Grandpa Newsome.

Momma rode up front with Grandpa Newsome and big mama rode in the back and laid me across her lap. The ride to the hospital was quiet, no one talked for a long time then Grandpa Newsome broke the ice and told mama that he would take care of the jailhouse situation while we went into the hospital. Momma thanked him and told him she would repay him. He told her for that one she owed him nothing because he would have done the same thing if he were in his shoes.

Big mama spoke and said, "A part of me agrees with you Mr. Newsome but two wrongs don't make no right. I want this nightmare to be over, but I don't want anybody else hurt. You know that boy unless you make him promise not to take matters into his own hands he won't stop until he serves justice on both them boys." "I know what you mean Rev. Hairston, I will definitely talk to him before I bring him home. Emma Mae, just incase I don't get through at the jailhouse before you get through at the hospital here is some cab fare. If it is not enough tell them, that I will pay them the rest tomorrow if they want to come by the house" said grandpa Newsome. "Thanks again." My mother said looking as if she were lost. "I know you have a lot to think about right now Emma Mae, but you focus on one thing at a time. That is why we are all family. You got all of us here together working to figure this maze out and we will get through this together. Now go and take care of my grandbaby," Grandpa Newsome said pulling up in front of the hospital.

Once inside the hospital, big mama found us some seats and momma went to the big desk to talk to the woman behind it. I couldn't hear what she was saying because it looked like she was whispering. Whatever she said made the lady turn red and she told her someone would be right with her. Momma came and sat beside us as the lady left the desk and went behind a door. We sat and we sat. Finally, they called my name. We all got up and followed the nurse behind the door and into a big hospital room. I had never seen a hospital before. It was smelly and there was a lot of screaming going on. I heard somebody saying push, push and there was a lot of screaming coming from behind the curtain. Then I heard a baby cry and a whole lot of people laughing. Big mama had a smile on her face, and I looked and so did my mother. Then I saw a doctor come from behind the curtain with a baby full of blood. I screamed and told big mama quick push the curtain closed. Momma and big mama started to laugh and didn't know why but it felt good to see them laugh after all those tears today. I laughed too.

It wasn't long before the doctor came in and looked at my face and started to ask questions like? "Who hit you with a baseball bat?" I didn't know any better, so I said my friend didn't hit me, she hit the boy and the boy had punched me in the nose." The doctor looked real confused and then he said, "Let's start from the beginning. Tell me what happened." I told him everything how it started and how it ended. He sent for a nurse and told me he would be right back. The nurse came in and asked my mother and big mama to leave the room, but my mother refused but big mama looked at me and I told her "Go ahead time for you to steal away and pray." She smiled as tears filled her eyes and she hurried out the room. The nurse looked all in my nose, down my throat. Up my butt and turned me every which way but loose. As soon as she left, I heard a voice from behind the curtain asking was I decent. "Yes!" Came my mother's reply and back came the curtain and there stood the police. "I have to ask you daughter some questions Mrs. Garnet is that all right with you." "I knew it would happen sooner or later," my mother said "but I am not going anywhere." "I don't blame you," said the policeman "if it was my daughter I wouldn't either."

Here I go again telling everything for the umpteenth time. But this time he had some new questions like how old was I? Who was the other boy? Did I see him attack my friend? Why were we looking for sticks? Just plain dumb questions but I answered them to the best of my ability. Then he told me I was one of the bravest six-year-olds he had ever met. It looked like it was crying time again because he reached for a tissue and so did my mother. Big mama never returned to the curtained room, and I got dressed and we went out front to the area where we started.

Sitting in the chair with his head on big mama's shoulder was my big brother, Vandie and when he saw me, he ran to meet me. He picked me way up high and then held me to his big chest and squeezed me so very tight. Then he whispered in my ear "Nobody is Ever going to hurt you again as long as I live. I promise you baby sister, I promise you." Well, he wouldn't put me down, he carried me to Grandpa Newsome's car and put me in the backseat beside big mama.

Then he stopped to hug momma, and she started to cry in his arms. "I'm sorry," he said "I don't want you ever to hurt behind me momma, but I just can't stand back and let some knuckled heads hurt my sisters or you. I'm the man of the house and a man's got to do what a man's got to do and I'm man enough to pay the consequences," Momma just cried and cried then my big brother opened the door and put her in the front seat, and he got in the back beside me. I leaned my head on my brother's arm and he put his arms around me and held me all the way home. I must have fallen to sleep because when I woke up Vandie was carrying me into the house.

That night was like a nightmare. My youngest brother was hold up at my Grandma Sallie's house and there was a lot of screaming about him coming home and facing the music. My grandma Levy was bound and determined to beat the black off him. My momma was angry, but she wanted to hear his side of the story and my grandmother Sallie was not letting anyone get close to him. My oldest brother, Vandie had gotten his thick belt out and voluntarily given it to grandma Levy. He was willing to walk her to Grandma Sallie's house and hold the boy down, and knock his head off if he reared up at her while she was getting her licks in on him. Big mama, well she retired early and was upstairs rocking me in her big rocking chair and covering my ears every now and then so I wouldn't hear all the swearing coming from the downstairs.

Let me pause here, my brother, Vandie, was the type that wouldn't hurt a fly. Literally he loved everyone and everything but when it came down to what was right and what was wrong, he amazed me. I remember he had done something wrong to my oldest sister. He came in the house confessing and carrying his own switches, telling my mother he deserved a whipping for what he had done and apologizing all at the same time. He loved music and spent a lot of time making a bass guitar so that he could join a band. He had skills and Grandpa Newsome knew that that was one reason he loved him so. He took him under his wing as a mentor and taught him carpentry and woodwork and he helped him make all sorts of things. His guitar was the greatest piece of work they had put together and everyone wanted him to play it. He never had lessons and yet he was a natural bass player. I admired him. For the most part he was a jokester and a pretty happy go lucky kind of fellow. So basically, unless you gave him reason to hurt you that wasn't his Method of Operation.

Well back to that night. I heard the door slam and then silence. Big mama must have become curious too because she eased me off her lap and ushered me to the bed telling me to wait quietly right there. I waited until she left the room and started down the steps and then I looked out the bedroom window. Going down the schoolyard was my grandma Levy and Vandie. But where was my mother? I heard what seemed to be crying in the kitchen, but I couldn't hear clearly from the bedroom. I had to go to the bathroom to hear through that floor over the kitchen.

So I crept to the bathroom. I couldn't hear well so I stood quietly with my ear to the wall, but I could not hear any talking just sobbing. I knew which steps squeaked so I purposely missed them as I moved from the bathroom to the stairs so that I could hear. Still no one was speaking, I started to believe I was home alone so I sneaked to the bottom of the steps and peeked into the kitchen and there at the table sat my mother and big mama both holding each other and both crying. The sight of them crying made me ill. My eyes hurt, my stomach hurt, my whole head hurt and it was all because I wanted to play with my friends and look for sticks. I wished someone would beat me with a stick now for all the pain I had caused my entire family. I sneaked back up the steps and went to bed and I cried silently into my pillow until I fell to sleep.

The next morning when I woke, I really believed someone had beaten me up in my sleep with a stick. My face hurt, my head hurt, my stomach was turning over and over again. I jumped up and ran to the bathroom. When I returned to the room. I noticed that no one was there. Not my sisters, nor my big mama, nor my mother so I went to the bathroom, washed up put my clothes on and ran downstairs.

It was a lovely day in the neighborhood. The sun was shining brightly, the sky was blue, and the birds were singing sweetly. I stood at the door looking out at the world as if I had a new pair of eyes. I heard voices coming from behind the house, so I walked to the side door and peered down into the yard. There stood my Grandmother Levy, big mama and my mother hanging up clothes on the clothesline. Grandma Levy was whistling, and big mama was humming, and Momma was singing, and they sounded so beautiful together. I was amazed because big mama was always annoyed when grandma Levy whistled because she said it wasn't lady like, but she could showoff whistle any tune you could name. Today it appeared that they were enjoying each other, and they looked beautiful together. I sat down on the steps and just listened. No one seemed to notice me, so I just sat quietly watching. Once that song ended my big mama started up another tune and my momma started to sing, and Grandma Levy started to whistle and then stop as though something had startled her.

Momma continued to sing, and big mama hummed but tears started to stream down Grandma Levy's eyes. I saw my mother look her way and she began to sing even louder and big mama looked at momma and then glanced at Grandma Levy. Then big mama moved over to her and put her arms around her. She boohooed in big mama's arms and momma kept singing. She sang so beautifully that I wanted to get up and shout and dance. For her singing made me feel like something inside me was making me move. Instead, I sat closing my eyes and rocking side-to-side feeling all warm inside. Then something strange happened big mama started praying and calling on the name of Jesus. I opened my eyes to see Grandma Levy, was now on the ground in front of big mama on her knees.

Momma kept singing big mama kept praying. Grandma Levy kept crying. She was crying so hard that I got scared that she was sick, and I started to get up and run to her but my feet felt like they were frozen, and my legs felt like lead so I couldn't get up. I wanted to speak but my lips felt like they had been glued together. Then I remembered what big mama said to me one time, she said, "Let the Lord have his way. Whenever God wants to draw you close to him, he knows the time and the place, and his spirit will make you yield no matter where you are." I believe it was Grandma Levy's yielding time.

Grandma Levy was a good woman, but she liked to party, drink beer and dip snuff all of what big mama said was a sin. I believe the Lord was using this time to clean her up, cause she sure couldn't go anywhere. She looked like "Raggedy Ann" all sprawled out on the ground. It seemed like a long time before my mother finished her song, but big mama was still praying and when she finished, she walked over to momma and hugged her and laid her hands on her head and stomach and prayed for her. I noticed for the first time that my mother's stomach looked like James' mother's stomach, which meant she was with child.

Grandma Levy was finally getting up off the ground and my feet came loose so I ran down the steps to help her up. I acted as though I hadn't seen anything and even asked her was she hurt. She smiled at me and said "I'm fine child just help me up please." I grabbed her hand, and she stood and gave meal hug. By now, big mama had stopped praying and momma was wiping her eyes on her shirtsleeve. I ran to big mama and said good morning as I began hugging her waist. She bent over and hugged me saying what a lovely day the Lord had given us. Then momma asked me for her hug and kiss and if I was hungry. She told me to go inside they would be in shortly.

I went inside and my brother Vandie was preparing four Mason jars with flowers. He had arranged them so beautifully. "Wow where did you get them?" I asked. "Quiet, you'll spoil the surprise. Mister Joe told me to pick them from his flower garden." He said. When he finished, he asked me to carry two of them into the living room and put them on the coffee table. I did and then he told me to go back in the kitchen and don't say a word to anyone. I did that too.

It wasn't long before the mothers came into the house, and they were happier than I had ever seen them. They washed their hands and started to gather food to cook for breakfast. Big mama sat down at the table and started to clean chicken for dinner while momma and grandma levy fixed eggs and sausage for breakfast. My brother strolled out of the living room as if he had just woke up and kissed each of them on the cheek. "Looks like we got some food," he said "when there's more than one cook in the kitchen I know we are on high times." He said. They all laughed. I was watching and enjoying the new atmosphere in the house. I couldn't remember how long it had been since I had seen them get along so well.

I knew they all loved each other because when times were rough, they always seemed to come together on one accord and make it through. Big mama would say they all drew from each other's strength, that not everyone was strong in all areas but there was always onto strongest when they needed to be and that gave encouragement to those who needed it. She to me she was always the strongest in every area, but she always gave encouragement and credit to whomever might need it at the times. I admired her and I always wanted to be just like her, and I was glad to be named after her for her memory would never die as long as I was around. Why was I thinking like that? I don't know but I know that I knew she would not always be around and as scary as that thought was, I felt comfort just because she had explained life to me, and I understood and what I didn't I knew I would understand it better by and by.

My sisters started to return one by one, and breakfast was about to be placed on the table. I put out the miniature plates and glasses and my brother confined everyone to the kitchen area so that they would not ruin his surprise. Everyone washed their hands in the kitchen sink and sat down at the table. After big mama blessed the food, we all sat down to eat. It was the greatest breakfast I had ever eaten. We laughed and joked and had a good time together as a family. Of course, my baby brother was missing and so was my other great grandma Sallie, but we had already expected that she wasn't one to get over things overnight, she kind of held grudges for at least a week. But I knew she would come around. When we had all finished breakfast Vandy said, "Ladies please stay seated and close your eyes." I closed mine too because I knew I was a lady in the making. He always called ladybug and me his little ladies. He walked out of the room and returned several times reminding us all not to peek and then he said open your eyes. Smiles and surprised expressions graced the faces of all my mothers. He gave a speech. "To the ladies of my life: May these flowers which are not as beautiful as you ladies symbolize my admiration and love for you all and show you that I am thankful and blessed with such loveliness in my life. May God bless and keep all of you forever, you are the loves of my life." He was quite a debonair and handsome young man as my grandma Levy would say. I was proud to have him as my brother. First, he gave big mama her flowers and kissed her hand then grandma Levy then momma. He knew the generation order and he respected that at all times. Big mama was always first even when momma was present. After he passed out those three Mason jars vases he still had three left and he passed my oldest sister one, then me, and then ladybug got one. Tears were flowing down the cheeks of everyone and that made me cry along with the fact I was allergic to one of the flowers and didn't have a clue which.

Grandma Levy declared this day to be family day and that we would play family games and eat snacks, it was the perfect day until about three o'clock. At three, great-grandmother, Sallie appeared with my knuckle headed brother. She had dressed him up and he had a haircut. He looked like a little angel. He showed no remorse and acted as though nothing had ever happened. Even though Grandma Levy asked him several times if he had anything he wanted to say to the family and especially to his sister. He never said a word and he never looked my way and while grandma Levy tried to make him, he stood quietly staring at the wall. Finally, my mother spoke and told him he was punished and that he could not join in family fun day, he had to go to his room. Momma asked big mama if she mind if they had a little fun today and maybe played cards. Big mama replied that they knew how she felt about cards but today she would be no stick in the mud so play to your hearts' content. Grandma Sallie and momma prepared the table to play cards, and big mama gathered me up to go to our room. I wanted to play cards too, but I knew that big mama thought that to be a sin, and me, also knew she had something wonderful she wanted to share with me.

I always will believe that spending time listening to her was better than any game that was ever invented. So I grabbed her hand and followed her upstairs. Once inside the room, she placed me on the side of the bed and pulled up her big rocking chair. Once she was comfortable, I jumped down from the bed and into her lap. "Baby let me tell you something about sorrow and forgiveness. When a person is Godly sorry for something he knows he has done wrong there is a special burden on his heart that will not allow him to rest until he has asked forgiveness. This is called conviction. Conviction will make a man realize that the ugliness he has done is not pleasing to God and he will hop at the chance to ask to be forgiven. No one has to make him, beg him or lead him. He will just feel sad in his heart, and he will want to. It's only if he wants to and he is obedient to the spirit that is leading him to ask in the first place. What your brother did was quite ugly and his part in the whole mess is yet to be revealed and so is his heart. For God looks at the heart of a man, and not at the outward appearance, you can put the finest of clothes on and still be a devil inside. Once God convicts his heart he will apologize on his own. Do you understand?" "No!" I replied. "Well, you may not understand it right now, but you will understand it better by and by."

Grandma Levy's vacation was about to end. She wanted us all to come to Grandma Sallie's house, where she had been staying to have a going away party. Big mama wasn't into parties, but she loved her grandbaby, and she never hid that fact. So, she agreed that this Saturday we would gather at Sallie's. Grandma Levy took us all shopping at the *Piggly-Wiggly* store. She told us to buy whatever we wanted. So Vandy, Tyra, and knucklehead went down one aisle filling a cart, while Ladybug and I stayed close to big mama, momma and grandma levy. I brought a plastic book bag and some candy. *Piggly-Wiggly* was glad to see grandma Levy. The cashier said they rolled out the red carpet for her because she always spent big money. I looked around at the floor and I didn't see any red carpet. But grandma Levy spent big money. She spent so much money that they had to call her a cab. We had so many groceries that everybody couldn't fit in the cab. So, the children walked back home while the mother's rode.

It was only a few blocks from the store to Sallie's, she lived right off the main street on a sloping street called Vine Street. It was always slick as glass summer or winter. I would get in the middle and take a running start and slide down the street when I wanted to have fun all the other times I would just slide.

Grandma Levy told us to hurry home so that we could help take the bags in the house. Tyra asked could she go to her friend's house one street over on Jones Street and knucklehead wanted to go with her. So, Grandma Levy told them not to stay long, she thought we could handle bringing in the bags without their help. We skipped and hurried home and got there about the same time the cab did. Vandy hustled up the hill to help open the car doors for the ladies. Mr. Pickles was driving, and he helped with the bags.

Grandma Levy handed ladybug and I a Popsicle and told us to sit on the water meter in front of Sallie's house and enjoy our Popsicles, we were too young to help. She reached in the cab, grabbed a bag, and handed one more to Sallie Lou and they headed for the house. We had just sat down to eat our Popsicles when momma came out the house to get another bag, she was smiling. She climbed inside the cab and grabbed a bag when all of a sudden, the cab took off down the street with nobody driving it. I stood up, dropped my Popsicle and started to scream as all of the mothers were coming out the house. The cab flipped upside down on momma and pinned her against the church wall.

Everybody was screaming and running down the hill. Grandma Sallie was the first one to get to the cab. Big mama was close behind her. Hollowing! **JESUS! JESUS! JESUS!** Vandy and Mr. Pickles were bringing up the rear and people from the main street were running to Vine Street. Grandma Levy was giving instructions to lift the car off momma. Big mama and Sallie Lou and Mr. Pickle's had already lifted the car and placed it on its side while Vandy and grandma Levy pulled mama to safety. I held ladybug back. She wanted to go to see about momma. But I knew I had to be the big sister and keep her from under our mothers' feet while they had work to do. So, I prayed and cried and covered my sister's face in my arms so that she couldn't see what was happening.

Quick as a flash, the ambulance was at the bottom of the street and so were the cameramen from the news. I saw "Scoop and Snoop". People were snapping pictures and talking to people as they placed momma into the ambulance. Grandma Levy climbed up in the front seat. Vandy ran behind the ambulance. Big mama, Sallie and Mr. Pickles came slowly up the hill. Mr. Pickles keep apologizing saying he should have gotten his brakes checked out. Well, big mama and Sallie just couldn't make it any further because they all but collapsed on the water meter. Sallie grabbed ladybug and big mama grabbed me, and they held us close and cried.

Once they got themselves together, they took us inside and told us to get up on the couch and take a nap. I don't know exactly when Mr. Pickles left. But big mama and Sallie Lou went upstairs. I heard big mama crying and I heard another voice crying too. I had never heard Sallie Lou cry before she was always so hard. But today she was crying and for the first time I heard her praying too. I never knew she could pray but being big mama's daughter, I should have known she could cause if big mama taught me, I am sure she taught her own child.

It took me a long time to go to sleep. I listened to big mama and Sallie Lou tag team the devil for a long time but when I woke, they were in the kitchen preparing food together. I walked in and asked would momma be, okay? Big mama told me to come close. She pulled up a chair and placed me on her knee. Sallie finished up and covered her pots and came to sit at her table too. I was scared to death.

"You know your momma is a strong woman. I remember when you were born, she was about to lose you and possibly die herself from losing so much blood. I remember how God made the white hospital take her and how Mr. Bo Skeets came to donate blood when they sent forth the call for his blood type." "Mr. Bo Skeets you mean that drunken man that was at church?" I asked. "Yeah, that drunken man that was at church is that man that saved your life and his blood is probably running through your veins." Sallie said laughing. I thought she was being mean but big mama shook her head in favor of what she had just said.

Big mama continued. "Mr. Bo Skeets hasn't always been a drunk. He was a good man. Fought in the war, was an electrician, broke horses and had a wife and children. I tell you all the time. You need to always be nice to people you don't never know what stage of life they are in, and you don't know what hand in life they've been dealt with. Mr. Bo Skeet's was and is a good man. He had a good wife and a good family; they were my husband's first friends when we came to this town. Mr. Bo Skeet's wife got caught in the T.B. epidemic, she had to go to the sanitarium, and she died. Later on, the plague came back and claimed my husband.

Mr. Bo Skeets tried to raise his children by himself, but it became too much for him, so he let them go and stay with his mother-in-law. She never brought them back and he could never find them. So, he became the town drunk and turned away from God. But God has a way of drawing a person back to him. He has never been in any trouble, and he has always kept his house in hopes his children would return. I believe one day they will cause he's on the right track now and God sees his heart.

But again, I say your momma is strong. This baby's going to make it through the rough times too." "Baby? Momma got a baby?" I questioned. "Well, what you think her stomach was poking out for?" asked Sallie "do you think she swallowed a watermelon whole." They both laughed a little. I was glad to see them laugh, and I wasn't about to ruin the mood with no smart aleck remark. "Your grandma Levy called and said that she had a "preemie." That means that the baby was born before it was time and will have to stay in the hospital for a while but she will be fine and will come home as soon as she gets strong enough.

I had just one more question burning inside of me, so I asked my mamas how was it they were the first ones to reach momma today when she was in trouble. Sallie said that she functioned on pure adrenaline. That when you see an accident of such life threaten nature you just get this extra strength out of nowhere that makes you do what has to be done. "Superwoman strength."

Big mama said that is what a true believer calls supernatural "Holy Ghost" power. She said that because she knew, trusted and believed God as the lover of her soul, the keeper of her mind and the mender of her heart that if He didn't spare my mother's life. He was still God worthy to be praised.

I was grateful and glad that God decided to spare my momma's life and to give me a new baby sister too!

CHAPTER 9

No Excuses

Romans 1:20-21
For the invisible things of hi from the creation of the world are
clearly seen, being understood by the things that are made,
even his eternal power and Godhead; so that they are without
excuse: because they knew God, they glorified him not as God
neither were they thankful; but became vain in their
imaginations, and their foolish heart was darkened.

"Big mama how do people know that God exist, if they don't have nobody to teach them and read to them like we do? How do they know to live for God?"

"Well, child that is a loaded question if I ever did hear one. One that I am not so sure I can possibly answer correctly. But let me give it a shot and when you are able to read God's word for yourself, pray earnestly for his guidance, understanding and wisdom then you will understand it better by and by."

"First, let me tell you a story. Once upon a time before man was created, before the sun and moon existed, before anything that was and is now existed, there existed a spirit named the great I AM. He said I AM that I AM. To believe HE existed before anything and everything is the foundation of faith and the core of Christianity. No man can understand every little thing about how God appeared on the scene as the young folks say but He was and always will be on the scene. He says He is the Alpha and the Omega, the beginning and the end. Therefore, if he was here first and he will be here last then he has no beginning and he has no end."

"Like a family tree!" I blurted out.

"What do you mean, baby, what about a family tree?"

"You remember when momma was asking about your family, she said she wanted to trace the family roots back to the beginning and make a book so that everyone could see who was in their family first and last."

"Well, you could look at it like a family tree if it will help you picture where I am trying to go okay!" She smiled shaking her head in acceptance.

"Okay big mama, Go on!" I said with excitement. I wanted her to finish her story, she always taught me something special.

She continued. "You know that God created by speaking everything that was and is: The light came, the sun, the moon, the stars, the animals, the earth, the planets, everything became real when God opened up his mouth and said let it be. We were created in his image so if we open up our mouths and ask then he gives us what we ask him for even revelation of him."

"Man can look around and see the evidence of existence and manifestation (real life) of God in everything. Everything created in the world should clearly be evidence of the existence of God and be appreciated as if it were a gift from God. Man is without excuse for not acknowledging God as his creator because everything that is and will be cries out, I am because God is.

In the days of old if man wanted to know God he would pray and ask for the revelation of His existence. If he prayed to the cow, sun, moon or other false Gods then he would see that they could not answer him. If he sought the true and the living God, then God would manifest himself in a way in which they could relate and in the culture that they could relate to. You see, God meets you at the point you are. He doesn't give you deep theology if you are a baby. He doesn't tease you with riches if he is not going to bless you. He first has to test you and then He has to bless you. Man has to understand that God has appeared in everything and as he controls everything no excuses can be made for not knowing of his existence. At times man has tried to make God out to be just another man, some worship the animals, moon and stars as if they were God, but God is not pleased. God looks for obedience, which is better than sacrifice.

Abraham was a man that endured quite a few tests. He had to leave the land, the family and the comfort that he knew and go to a place where he did not know and around people where he knew nobody. He had to have the test of faith when God promised him a son and even when he messed up by not waiting long enough for the promise God granted mercy and the promised son. Then when he received the promise God tested him to kill his promised son. By faith Abraham lifted up the knife to destroy the long-awaited promise but because God saw his faithfulness and obedience, he spared the son and supplied a ram instead. You see, God can manifest himself in any way, form or fashion he wants too.

He gave Moses the tablet of commandments that said that thou shall have no other God's before me and that thou shalt not make any graven images or anything to stand in God's place for He was a jealous God. Testing the spirits is one way the Bible tells us that we can try them and see if they are, from God.

Now I am not talking about voodoo and witchcraft and all that other forbidden and already proven evil spirits. I'm speaking about people and prophecy that comes forth from those who claim to be of God and prove that they are no more than wolves in sheep clothes. You have to watch the fruits that they bear, by fruits I mean, the way that they live, and the foundations that they lay. Test the words that they say, line them up with the word of God.

Search the scriptures, see what is real and what is fable and a way to false teaching. Oh, my child, when you grow old enough to understand. I pray daily that God will give you wisdom and courage to line up on his side. Take the word and apply it to your heart, mind and soul. Be wise enough to discern what is godly, true and profitable for your soul and be courageous enough to walk away from false teaching, poor leadership and wrong motives. That God will be guidance for your existence, that he will nurture your talents, set his hand of favor on your life and let your light shine brightly before all generations to come as guidance in the flesh." Big mama sounded as though she was praying, and she looked like it too as she laid her hand upon my head and closed her eyes and spoke over my head.

Well, I sat there real quiet, almost afraid to move and I watched as she fought back the tears. They were tears of joy I could tell that because big mama very seldom had tears of sadness. She told me that before, she said every day that she lived she found something to be happy about even when life would be unhappy. She said that there always will be a time to be happy and a time to be sad, but don't let sad rule yah. Take the time to be sad, but when sad done run its course, get on the course of happy and stay there. Find something good in everything. Cause God takes every bad thing and works it around to be good. Well, I let her get her prayer through and I said hallelujah and amen. She looked at me and smiled and tried to return to her story.

"Well, where was I?" she asked me. "You were talking about testing man's fruits." I said she smiled and said "You sure have such a great memory and wisdom for such a young child. That is why I know in my heart that God is going to be glorified with your life as you learn to live for him. Thank you, Jesus!" She mumbled and smiled.

"Anyway, as I was saying, as man unfolds his hand, you can learn whose side he really is on. Phony men and women have a way of not always being able to remember a lie and allowing their lifestyle to contradict or be otherwise different from what they say as a posed to how they live. Listening carefully, watch cautiously and pray reverently is a necessity because as a spiritual human being, you can only believe some of what you hear, 1/2 of what you see and all of what God says. Man has a way of telling you that this is right and that is wrong and then you see them partaking in wrong and you get confused. Because they supposed to be representing God and now you get confused about

God. Well, the arm of flesh will fail you. God is not the author of confusion. If he says man shall not live by bread alone but by every word that proceeds from the mouth of God, then that is what He means. No Indian giving. Now I am not being mean about no Indian because you know I'm partly one. But God don't give you anything to later come and take it back. For the blessings of the Lord makes you rich. And adds no sorrow with it.

Not one of God's servants has ever walked a hundred percent pure before God with the exception of (Enoch) and JESUS and we know that Jesus was human filled with the spirit of God (God's son) so we won't count him as born of woman and man, but woman and the spirit of God. Enoch was pleasing to God and walked with God and God took him before he could be totally contaminated by lust of the eyes, the lust of the flesh and the pride of life.

Anyway, man has to understand that God has appeared in everything and as he controls everything no excuse can be made for not knowing of his existence. Even without a Bible just like you are asking me about God somewhere around this world right now someone is asking about God.

Man's curiosity is just not to kill a cat but to kill the uncertainty of the existence of a true and living God. God's mercy and grace spares until man has revelation and opportunity to either, feel, witness, experience or desire to obtain the truth and acknowledge his existence. It may never occur the way we have been blessed to have obtained it through good teachers, the Bible and the Holy Spirit but it is real, and God will in no way turn away anyone who seeks him. So, people have to have the will to live in search of truth and in search of holiness and in search of God.

Man's spirit was created with a worshipping presence and no man has an excuse for not giving God a thought, a thank you or tithe (talent, treasure, time). That is why I always teach you that putting God first makes you stop and consider what is right and what is wrong, when you know God sees and knows and is everywhere and pleasing him is all that matters. Well, I hope that I have answered your question." I shook my head as if I fully understood but my big mama knew me best, she said, "If I haven't, explained to your complete understanding if you will just meditate on these things I have said. Learn to be a good listener in church, learn to read the word of God, search the scriptures, memorize them and pray, and seek knowledge through good books. Surely you will understand in better by."

CHAPTER 10

Let Not Your Heart Be Troubled

John 14:1-3
Let not your heart be troubled: ye believe in God, believe also in me. In my father's house are many mansions: If it were not so, I would have told you. I go to prepare a place for you. And if I go and prepare a place for you, I will come again, and receive you unto myself; that where I am, there you may be also. And whither I go ye know, and the way ye know.

The weather had changed, and it had started to get rather breezy out. It was a good thing too because ever since the playground incident, big mama always was outside while I played, and she was getting quite under the weather so to speak. At night, I heard her cough and blow her nose continuously. It was quite noticeable. Momma had suggested several times that she see the doctor and she had told her that it was just a cold that had to run its course. However, momma didn't want it to run her house and everyone else into the hospital so late one evening she demanded that big mama see a doctor or not come around us and the new baby.

Big mama must have been really sick because she agreed. Momma immediately went next door to call doctor Hickman. He made house calls. Momma was really concerned, and she must have been quite convincing because before she could get back into the house good doc was at the door. He loved my big mama, and he never hid his concern either. "Where is she?" he asked. "Upstairs." My mother pointed the way. Up the stairs, he flew with his black bag in toe. I was right behind him but once I got to the top of the stairs, he told me that I had to wait outside the door. He must have been in there for hours at least it seemed like it. When he came out, he said, "She can have visitors now!" Smiling at me. I didn't even wait for him to move. I said excuse me and jumped up on the bed with big mama. I heard doc go down the steps and into the living room to talk to momma but today I didn't feel much like ease dropping, I was going to get the news straight from the "horse's mouth".

"What did the doctor say and be honest with me I can take it." I said as if I was a real grownup. "Well, it wasn't the news I was looking for, but it wasn't the worst either. I'm pretty sick, I have pneumonia. He heard it in my lungs and chest so that means I will be out of circulation for a while but that also means I will need somebody to take care of me." My eyes started to water, and I got scared again. I felt so uneasy because I had to leave her and go to school every day, it had just started a few months ago and I was now in the second grade. Momma had to work, and nobody would be at home to take care of my big mama. I sat quietly trying to think of what to do.

"Baby sister I need you to come and wash the dishes." called momma. "I'll think of something I told big mama I'm going to take care of you, and you can take that to the bank." I told her as I leaned over to kiss her check, before I jumped off the bed. She was as hot as fire. I jumped down the steps and into the kitchen just in time to see doc headed for the door. "Doc! Excuse me sir please. My big mama is really hot. But she is not sweating, and she has all that cover over her. Is there something I can do?" I asked him.

"Well, there is something you can do. Do you mind Emma Mae if she goes with me to my car?" "No that will be fine, get your jacket off the rack baby it's turning cold out there!" Momma said. We walked down the steps and to the fancy car parked in the backyard. "Listen, I know you are really close to your big mama, and I know she loves you dearly. She needs to drink plenty of liquids, juice, water, tea, soup, and Jell-0, whatever you can get her to eat. She is dehydrated that means she needs to get minerals in her system so that it will operate right. You got to get her to do that. Do you think you can get her to do that?" "I sure can!" I said with a positive smile. "I believe you can. Listen. She needs some TLC and this medicine every 4 hours." He instructed as he grabbed a brown bottle of what looked like cough syrup. "Do you know how old your big mama is?" He asked me. "Eighty something! I said with a smile. "Yes, she is. He said that's a lot of years, isn't it?" He asked me. "It sure is." I said proudly. "Well, we want her to stay around a while longer so with a little TLC, medicine and prayer she should be able to do that. "Do you pray?" he asked me. "Yes, sir I do." I answered. "Well do double time. Here take this medicine and run along back to take care of big mama." I thanked him again and started up the steps and as I looked back, he had taken off his glasses and started to wipe his eyes sort of like he was crying. Then he placed his glasses back on his face and got into his car.

I ran in the house and told my mother that big mama had to take the bottle every four hours and that she needed to have juice, water, tea, Jell-o and TLC every four hours. I washed my hands and went into the refrigerator to look for juice and asked momma to make the tea, the Jell-O and the potato soup. Then I asked my mother where I could find the TLC. She must have noticed that there was a panic in my spirit, and it must have been one in hers too because she stopped me and pulled me close to her and I burst into tears. She walked me to the table where she sat down and put her arms around me and let me cry. I don't know how long I cried but it must have been a long time, but I felt so much better. I believe it was the first time I can remember my mother holding me and just letting me cry. Until now it was always big mama that I ran to when I fell down or got my feelings hurt but today, I had a special connection with my mother.

I must have cried too long, because when I looked up, big mama was standing in the doorway and momma was not happy to see her downstairs. "What on Earth is wrong with my baby?" She asked. "You shouldn't be down here. You need to be back in bed." momma said. "I would rather lie on the couch by the stove. Can I just get some heat? Now what's wrong with my baby?" Big mama asked. I wasn't going to lie but for some reason I wasn't going to tell either. "I'm fine." I said. "I need to wash the dishes and get you some juice for the medicine doc left for you to take. Now please go and lay down." I must have sound real convincing, or she was really weak because she went straight to the living room and curled up on the couch.

Vandy must have known she was going to want to lie on the couch because he had already made it up like a bed and he brought her an extra blanket and tucked her in like a little child. He sure knew how to take care of us and most of the time it was like he knew what we were thinking even before we said anything. He was the greatest brother a person could ask for and believe me he was the man of the house. Momma made big mama hot tea with rock candy. I waited in the kitchen for my big sister to heat the dishwater. When momma left the kitchen, I asked her what we were going to do about big mama and getting her better. "Well," she whispered, "You know mom has to work and everybody has to go to school but if you really want to know what Vandy and I have decided maybe if you promise not to tell we can work this plan together." I crossed my heart and promised. "I am going to stay home tomorrow which is Thursday and Friday, I am going to be sick, I feel like I am coming down with something. If she is not better by Monday, momma is off then if she is not better by Tuesday Vandy will stay home Tuesday and Wednesday. Now this is where you come in if she is still not better then you stay home Thursday and Friday of next week. I am sure she will be better by then but if she's not then you have to step up to the plate and do what you can."

I was trying to achieve perfect attendance this year and I promised my teacher, as did all the other students that we would try to be there every day and on time. But I remembered what big mama had told me that sacrifice is required sometimes to attain something that you really want. I was willing to sacrifice my perfect attendance to make sure big mama was never left alone.

Even when she wasn't feeling up to par, big mama would tell me a story. Today was the story about good secrets and white lies. Good secrets were things that happened that no one but you and a friend could talk about because some people would never understand you unless they were the type of person that understood your heart. Secrets were kept hidden between people that had things in common. There were good secrets that required you to be loyal to a person and uphold their honor or name. Her story went like this.

You had a friend who asked his master for a chicken to feed his family. Let's say your friend had worked for this man and his family for years and today your friend didn't have any food to feed his family. He asks the master for one chicken and the master says no. Well, the master has about fifty chickens in the yard, and he tells this friend. Now your friend has about ten children at home to feed and they haven't eaten a good meal in days and the master ain't paid the man not one red dime but he ain't about to give him one chicken either. Well, your friend steals a chicken, takes it home and feeds his family.

"First of all, stealing is against the Word of God and every man should live by faith and if your friend was living by faith then God would have provided for his family, right?" She was asking me if I thought 'stealing' in this case was right. I answered I wasn't sure. "Well," she continued, "You know your friend stole the chicken but if you tell then you know that the master will beat your friend or far worse sell his family, so you have got to keep the secret if you want your friend to live and keep his family. Well, what would you do?" "I would keep the secret, and I would pray that the master didn't miss not one chicken or ever find out my friend stole from him." I said hoping I was right.

"Good answer," she said, seemed to agree. "But what if the master found out that the chicken was missing and that everybody was going to get a beating until someone told who it did then would you keep a secret?" "No, I ain't going to take no beating for somebody else's trouble." I told her, smiling and believing I had made the right decision. I know it sounds like a hard question to answer but it is how life is sometimes you have got to face some hard decisions. One thing that would help you out is that first off.

"You got to weigh the circumstances. This man worked and never got paid, he was an honest man. He went to the master and asked for a basic necessity and truly he had earned it. He needed to feed his children and knowing he may risk his life for something as little as a chicken. "Well, I hope he found the fattest one on the yard!" I interrupted! Big mama smiled and continued. "He had to do what was needed and necessary. Only you and your friend knew who stole the chicken and now everyone was subject to a beating until someone told the truth. Now some secrets people take to their grave because people are more important than chickens. Stripes heal and tears dry up. Families build ties that bind and never break because blood is thicker. Friends and people who are true to the bond of friendship sometimes take on the burdens of others and weather the storm when it's a matter of life hanging in the balance.

We know that little white lies are just as bad as big black ones. Sometimes it's best to shut your mouth and let your actions do the talking. Bad secrets will shake the very foundation of your soul. They give you uneasiness in your spirit like you can't rest and you know something is wrong. Usually that kind of secret has a small and seemingly harmless lie attached to it but a big black cloud of sin hovering around it. It's like an innocent baby that has no one to turn to, to confide in, it is the type of thing that if you told someone it would seem so far-fetched to them that they wouldn't believe you and you would be like a liar to them. That's what you watch out for. When someone asks you to keep a bad secret and they tell you no one will believe you if you tell, then that is when you tell and don't stop telling, until someone hears you with their heart.

Secrets are sometimes the strongest bond between real friends. Just know deep down what consequences you are willing to face and what you are not willing to face before you commit to a secret. Remember that little white lies lead to big black ones and they are never ever any good or good for nothing." She left me wondering if the Holy Ghost told her about my secret plans. Well even still my decision was made. Before I risked her wasting away or being alone and going to any early grave like my mother said. I was willing to miss a day or two of school and play just so that I could keep an eye and ear out for big mama.

It was a long time before big mama started to improve. It was a couple of weeks before I even wanted to go outside, to play, but big mama insisted that I go to the annual "Tom Thumb" rehearsals.

The "Tom Thumb" wedding was probably the biggest event we had to look forward to every year. Every year it was held at the same church and the same ladies did the organization of the program. Every year the children would come and hope that they would get picked as the Tom Thumb queen and king. It was my second year participating and I didn't like it last year. I thought that Mrs. Adams was very mean and unfair from what I witnessed last year. However, this year I was in for a really good lesson on unfairness.

It was a Friday evening, and the church was packed with children. I saw so many of my friends from school and the neighborhood that I had a hard time finding a seat because I wanted to sit by everybody. I loved my friends, and my friends loved me, so they called me from one side of the room to the other and like a sheep headed for the slaughter I blindly moved from one friend to the next. I barely heard Mrs. Adams when she announced the reason for us being there. I knew why I was there so I kind of blanked her out and continued to talk to my friend Jasmine.

I never noticed Mrs. Adams walking down the aisle towards me but I certainly felt her fingernails as they dug into my neck. "Ouch you're hurting me!" I exclaimed. "Well now that I have your attention, I just want to let you know that we are not here for you to run from one spot to the next. Come follow me!" She said. I would have followed her except she didn't let my neck go so it was more like come let me drag you to the front. It got quiet as all eyes were on me being dragged to the front seat. "Now sit right here, keep your mouth closed and pay attention to what we adults have to say." I started to cry not so much from the pain in my neck as it was because I was embarrassed. She had sat me beside my friend James. James and I had known each other since we were babies crawling around together. He reached over and grabbed my hand and whispered, "you're going to be all right." So, I stopped crying and squeezed his hand back and said thanks.

Mrs. Cotton was the other adult in charge. She showed genuine love with a smile and hugs and never said a whole lot, always letting Mrs. Adams lead. She was a heavyset, dark-skinned lady who was always nice and pleasant to everyone.

Let me shed some light on Mrs. Adams right here. Mrs. Adams had been planning and executing this event for years. She was about 5ft. 9 in real light skinned, long brown hair, real thin and real mean. She was the type that would see you on the street and cross to the other side to keep from speaking. Yet you always found her up in church planning and executing something special for the poor children in the city. Bragging about how much time she spent giving to poor families and the church. She was large and in charge. The greatest example of a hypocrite I can remember.

Finally, Mrs. Adams stopped bragging and giving instructions. She said she was doing something a little different this year to be fair to all the children. This year she was not picking a queen and anyone who had been a king or queen before was not eligible to be a queen or king this year. The first order of business was to separate according to age. So, I had to move back a couple of rows and James was right beside me, which made me feel better. Next, they separated the boys and the girls into the newly formed groups and Mrs. Adams came to every group and picked a king. The king was supposed to pick a queen from his age group and then we would get our lines for the play according to whoever was left. Jasmine and I waited patiently for her to choose our king. Jasmine was a pretty girl light skinned, long curly black hair and real nice. We had been friends since head Start and we played together as often as we could. Mrs. Adams picked James to be the king of our group and told him he had to choose his wife carefully because he would have to live with her forever. James smiled and said I will.

Mrs. Adams announced that our time was short this week and our time together was just about up. So, every boy was to look over the girls in his group and think about them the whole week and next Friday he could choose whom he wanted for his wife. Until then he was to keep it a secret. Ella, Linda and Freda were not eligible to be queen in our group because they had been queens before over the years. So, there were just five of us left for James to choose. I was glad rehearsal was over early. I wanted to get back to my house and check on my big mama. I had more important things to do than sit around and believe I was going to get married. I had been in phony wedding before and was never chosen for the wife or even the maid of honor.

I was already getting a little tired of this make-believe stuff that only the adults seemed to enjoy because as far as it looked to me most of the children were like me, they were irritated by Mrs. Adams' squeaky voice, phony walk and mean spirit and we didn't care who married whoever anyway.

Momma was working really steadily now, and she still allowed us to participate in after school and church programs, but she wasn't always able to pick us up. Today my big sister came to pick up Ladybug and me. James' older sister, who was my sister's friend, came to pick him up so we walked home together. James was always quiet, but he was unusually quiet now. I had been his friend forever and I knew him well if he was told to keep a secret, he was like Fort Knox besides I was his friend always and if he didn't choose me, I believe I could live with that or at least I hoped I could.

On Saturday my mother took us to the movies and Sunday we had dinner at Sallie Lou's house. So, I didn't have a chance to talk to James. But Monday morning, just like clockwork, he was standing at the end of the playground waiting for me to walk me to school. We had been in the same class since we started to go to school. James had walked me to school since we stopped riding the bus and our parents had stopped walking us to our new school last year. He always walked close to traffic and held my hand. We weren't boyfriend girlfriend or nothing, it was just that we had special care for each other. We got teased a lot, but we didn't care because at the end of the day you couldn't find two people closer than he and I. We went together like peanut butter and Jelly.

As we walked back past James's house his mother stood on the porch greeting me with her usual hey baby sis, have a great day and look after my baby boy phrase. As usual my response was. Have a great day too and don't worry, I'll take good care of him.

Walking with James was always pleasant until we got to the middle of Jones Street. That is where we would always encounter our daily enemy, a girl named, Drusilla we called her Dracula when she couldn't hear us. She was a bully, mean and nasty, she would lie, steal and hit you even if you hadn't done anything to her. She was the type who would throw a rock and then hide her hand. Dracula cursed like a demon, was fat and homely and she didn't like James or me. Sometimes I wondered. Was that the reason we held hands so that she wouldn't notice us shaking as we ran as fast as we could past her house. This morning was no exception there she stood on her front porch shaking her fist and saying I'm going to get y'all just wait and see. By the time she had finished stuttering the words out we had run past her house and to the corner for the safety of our crossing guard Mrs. Engle.

Mrs. Engle was probably one of the sweetest, caring and loving people in the whole world. She always greeted us with a smile, a hug and a God bless. If it were just James and I, then she would wait for more children to gather before she crossed us unless she noticed Dracula coming. Then she would cross us and make Dracula wait for the next group of children, which meant that by then James and I would be halfway to school. That's why I always felt safe with Mrs. Engle, it's like she had a radar detector out that keeps us from all kinds of danger, just not traffic only.

Once we had crossed over to the other side of Bland Street, we had just a couple of blocks to go before we were at school. I was dying to ask James if he had chosen a wife, but I knew if he wanted me to know he would tell me.

It seemed like Friday would never come but finally we were just moments away from rehearsal. As we sat in our assigned groups waiting for Mrs. Adams to finish her long-drawn-out speech. I glanced over at James; he gave me a big wide grin and I knew in my heart I was his choice. First Mrs. Adams went to the nine/ten-year-old and asked Albert Brownlow whom he had chosen. He chose a girl named Kenya who was a very pretty light-skinned girl with a big wide grin. She was very nice, and I remembered her being kind to me on several occasions when I was sad. Then she went to the seven /eight-year-olds. Freddy Sticks was the chosen king, and he had picked of all people Dracula's sister. Now Dracula's sister was quiet and shy, and she was kind of cute, but it still left to your imagination had Dracula cohered him into picking her sister she was such a bully. Next, it was our group, the five /six-year-olds.

James was now standing ready to announce his choice and just as I had suspected he had chosen me. I stood and walked proudly up front to stand beside my man. But my heart was full as my big mama would say and understand so as I approached the front I started to cry. I really don't understand why I started to cry, maybe it was because I knew what a friend James was to me or maybe it was because I knew how proud my family would be to see me as the queen. Whatever reason it was, I started to cry. When I arrived in front of the room and turned to face the other children, Mrs. Adams said, "What in the world are you crying for? You don't want to be the queen, well go back and sit down." I tried to explain that it wasn't that I didn't want to be the queen, I really didn't know why I was crying. "Well let me let you in on a secret, there are plenty of young ladies in your group willing to take your place and if you can't act as though you are grateful and straighten up your face then I will have no other choice but to choose someone else." I was literally shaking in my boots. I was hurting now more than ever. How dare she not only acted as though I couldn't have any feelings and threaten to replace me at my moment of weakness. She was just highly insensitive. I tried to regain my composure. Mrs. Cotton handed me a tissue and whispered, "Wipe your eyes and take in a deep breath, I understand." I took the tissue, said thank you and breathed deeply. Mrs. Adams started the instructions and started to pass out the scripts to all the participants. She informed us that we only had three weeks to learn our parts and that she would not accept any mistakes because her production was going to be excellent this year and anyone who was not willing to give an excellent performance should immediately step down.

We practiced for about another hour and then we were dismissed. As parents came to pick up children, James' sister and my sister again came to pick us up. I was ecstatic trying to tell my sister I was going to be the queen. She was so proud and so was James' sister. We walked up the street holding hands as we usually did and talking nonstop to each other. James asked me did I ever have any doubt that he would choose me and I kind of told him a little. "However, if you had chosen anyone else, I would have still been your friend." We laughed and joked all the way home. To me it was the greatest moment of my young life. I ran to tell big mama what had happened and was bursting at the seams to tell momma about it when she came home. Big mama told me she wouldn't miss this wedding for all the tea in China and she didn't do weddings, so I felt really special because she didn't go to the Jones Street church either and that is where the wedding was being held. I never really questioned why she never wanted to attend that church because it was at the bottom of our street. She went to the church in the middle of Jones Street from time to time when they had special occasions and sometimes, she even went across town to other churches, but she never went to the church at the end of the street. When momma finally got home from work, I hurried up and told her about me being selected as queen. She tried to be excited, but she was too tired. I could see it in her eyes so just told her I loved her and went to bed.

Saturday, James, Jasmine and I played on the schoolyard. We loved it that our parents were so close, because we could go to each other's house and on the weekend, we could play together all day. Today was just an ordinary Saturday and we were sitting down on the schoolyard steps trying to figure out what game we were going to play next when out of nowhere came Albert Brownlow. Albert lived in a nice big house right on the back of the playground. The only time I had been to his house was for trick or treat and I had never been inside, but it was good to see him twice in one week. Because we never saw much of him, we forgot he existed until he pops up.

He hardly ever came out to play, he was quiet when he did, and we had heard he was sick all the time. Albert was quite handsome, polite, dark, slim and tall. He was the type of fellow that when his mother called, he answered the first time and if she said come home, he ran without hesitation no matter how much fun he was having. I think all of us really liked him even though as I said he never played with us much but there was something about him that made him different. Something mystical and magical about how he walked and talked. He asked us if it was all right if he joined us in whatever game we were playing and immediately we all said yes as soon as we figure out what game we wanted to play. It was like we were all on the same page and spoke the same sentence so that made us all laugh.

Albert sat down with us and started talking. He asked us what games we had already played. I said everything we could think of, then he asked us if we had played hopscotch. We looked at each other and asked him how did you play hopscotch? Smiling, he jumped off the steps started looking around the ground. We all stood up and asked him what he was looking for. Something to make a hopscotch board with, like a piece of coal or something. We all started to look. James found a nice big piece of coal and Albert drew large squares on the schoolyard pavement. Then he told us each to find a rock and that the object of the game was to hop from one block to the next one foot two feet until we reached the top turn around and come back without falling and without stepping on any blocks that had a rock in it. If we fall, we had to start over. He demonstrated and we began to take turns. We were having a great time laughing and trying to keep our balance on one foot. I think we all liked the game. After about four or five games Albert began to look funny. He told us that he had to sit down so we all sat down on the steps. He held his head down between his legs and started to breathe funny. He was scaring me and I keep asking him was he all right. He shook his head no and quick as a flash, James got up and ran to get his mother.

Mrs. Brownlow came running up to the steps, with a small spray can in her hand. Albert breathed in it and laid back on the step. I was scared stiff and so was Jasmine. I had never seen anyone have an asthma attack. Mrs. Brownlow sat on the step directly behind him and gently rubbed his back and held his head in her hands. About five minutes went by before Albert began to breathe normal. She thanked James for quickly coming to get her. We all sat quietly. Mrs. Brownlow was the first to speak. She told us Albert had asthma and that sometimes even with normal playing he would become short of breath. She also told us that he stayed in the house during the spring and fall because the pollen on the trees made him sick. Today she made an exception to let him come out because he wanted to be with good friends.

Then Albert spoke. He told us how he always wanted to have friends like us that played so nicely together and shared everything with each other. He told us how he looked from his bedroom window every day for months as we played together and wished he could have the energy we had to do all the things we did. He even told us that he had never ever climbed a tree. He said he read a lot and that he had a special book that he read every day called the ***Our Daily Bread*** and that if we wanted to come to his house some time and play with him, he would share it with us. When he had finished, his mother asked him was he feeling well enough to walk on his own. He said he thought he did but when he stood up, he almost fell down. So, James got on one side, and I got on the other and he put his arms around our shoulders, and we walked him home. We walked slow and kept asking him did he need to stop and rest all the way to his house. Once inside Jasmine and Mrs. Brownlow propped pillows up on the couch and made him comfortable.

I can't speak for anybody else, but I was very nervous. I asked to use the restroom and as I came out James was standing at the door to go in, he looked nervous too, so we smiled at each other as we passed. Jasmine was sitting in the living room looking at the special book Albert had told us about, so I joined her standing, looking over her shoulder. When James came out of the bathroom he joined us in the living room, he sat beside Jasmine on the small couch. Mrs. Brownlow brought us all a piece of pound cake. Albert wanted us to stay a little while longer, and to tell you the truth I was ready to run out of there because I wasn't sure he was really alright, he still was breathing kind of funny. But James and Jasmine had gotten comfortable on the small couch and told me to come on and sit down because there was still more room. It was a real nice, comfortable couch. It was the best house I had ever been in. They had a floor model television. Two couches, a bookshelf, a record player and nice paintings on the wall, it was clean and smelled really fresh. Albert's mother was a nurse at the local hospital, and she made some great pound cake not as good as my great grandma's sweet corn bread cake, but it was running a close second.

Jasmine, James and I were all six going on seven and Albert was already nine going on ten. I guess that is why we never really knew him because he was older and because he was always sick. After looking through the pictures in the special book Albert asked one of us to read that day's message. We all wanted to read just like in class. We all three were great readers so we had no trouble reading. I loved to read but not without my glasses and I never played in my glasses, so I let James and Jasmine hash that one out. Just like the true man James was, he let ladies go first and Jasmine shonuff read that word. It was like she was preaching on Sunday. By the way, we all went to Sunday school together every Sunday too! It must have been a coincidence that the daily word was on friends. She read *John 15:13 no greater love has a man than this that he lay down his life for a friend.* Then she read a short story that told about friendship. It was a rather touching story, and we were just sitting there thinking. Then Albert asked us what we thought it meant, but before we could think about it and answer his mother told us that she thought Albert needed to rest and that any time we wanted to come over she would be pleased to have us. Being the type of man James was, he stood and thanked her for the cake, shook Albert's hand; lead us to the door, opened it, and waited for us to come out. We said our goodbyes and started back towards the playground.

I don't think any of us felt much like playing. So, we sat almost in a daze on the steps. It seemed like half the day had passed and we heard my mother call us in for lunch. I guess the good thing about our parents being so close was they went from house to house on the weekend and wherever they were is where we stayed all day. Everyone was at my house today and big mama could shed some light on the message we read today, and I couldn't wait to ask her.

Once we got cleaned up for lunch, big mama sat us down at the kitchen table blessed the sandwiches and headed back up the steps. I knew what that meant, that she was not in approval of whatever the grown-ups were doing in the living room. Mostly they were just playing cards and probably sneaking a drink hid outside in the front yard I bet. For the most part momma respected big mama she wouldn't dare drink in front of her or let liquor be in the house while she was there. She knew big mama didn't like for her to play cards and usually when it was momma's turn to entertain, big mama would give her space and leave and visit a friend for the day. But big mama had been under the weather lately and she was still a little weak, so she just decided to go to her room, read the word and come down later and sprinkle holy oil all over the place after everybody left.

I told my friends that my big mama was a preacher. She knew the word backwards and forwards. She was one of the wisest women in the world and if they really wanted to hear the truth about the word we read today, all we had to do was get big mama to set down and tell us a story. I told them that I would ask big mama about the message, and they were excited about getting the answer. So after lunch we all claimed we needed to go upstairs to the bathroom before we went back outside to play. So we all headed up the steps. Nobody was watching us so I softly knocked on big mama's door. "Come in" she replied so we all tiptoed into the bedroom.

I was quite embarrassed about my bedroom it was so crowded. Even though it was a huge room with two beds it was the room where everybody sleeps but it was always clean and neat and big mama said that's what counted the most.

"Big mama, we need to ask you about a word we read in a book call "*Our Daily Bread*." Her face must have brightened up like a shining star. "Do you think me and my friends could get a little bit of your time so that you could help us understand what this word means?" I asked. I loved to talk like. Like she was a real busy lady, and it made me feel really good to share her wealth of knowledge with my friends, besides she was to me the smartest, wisest lady in the whole world.

"Now baby girl you know I always have time for you and your friends come on in and y'all pull up a chair or better yet y'all sit up on the bed and I'll pull up my Bible and my rocking chair." Jasmine and I hopped up on the bed and James helped her pull over her rocking chair and get her Bible before he hopped up excitedly on to the bed in the middle.

"Well, my children, what did the message say?" she asked. Jasmine was truly the most excited I had ever seen her. "It was the word for today out of the book called *Our Daily Bread* and it was John 15:13." She smiled confidently she had a great memory. Big mama first went to the scripture. Then she had a book inside her Bible, and she turned to it and started to read. It was the same exact story Jasmine read. Big mama had the special book that Albert had *Our Daily Bread* book. We sat in amazement, and I asked, "How did you get Albert's special book?" "Baby girl when they made the book they didn't just stop at one. It is a special book though." We all laughed because we could relate to that when we were in reading circle everybody had the same book.

"It's called a daily devotional book that means it's a book that a person would use daily to spend time with God's word. It is a time for one to sit down and to take the time to think about God's word using a story and then looking over your life to see how it applies or can be applied to your life. In other words, how does the word of God fit into your life from that passage of scripture?"

"To better understand this scripture let's read verse 12 through 17." I jumped down and ran to the dresser to get my glasses and my bible so that we could sit on the bed and share. Big mama found the Chapter for us, and we placed the Bible on James' lap in the middle of us so that we could share. It was our first home bible study class, and I wondered were my friends feeling as special as I felt. From the looks on their faces, definitely yes!

Since Jasmine was on the end closest to big mama and since she was company, she read first then James and then me. When we had finished, big mama started to explain what we had read. "You see, Jesus was talking with his disciples. Do you know what a disciple is?" We all shook our heads no. "Well, I know all of you know who Jesus is because I see y'all in Sunday school. Since you know that Jesus came into the world to save the world from sin by paying the penalty for all mankind's sin by dying. He was really laying down his life on the cross so that all might have the right to eternal life. Then in order for everyone to be able to know what his purpose was, and his message was, he had to train people to carry the message of salvation from one generation to the next. In order to do that, he had to choose people he could trust, depend upon and feel comfortable with. His disciples were not just people he was training to do a job, but they were his friends. Guys that hung out all the time together, ate over each other's houses, shared their deepest secrets with each other, told stories, read the word together looked out for each other no matter what the cost. They really loved one another and were willing to fight even unto death for one another if need be. Like you three musketeers." We all smiled.

"Jesus was commanding them to love one another as he had loved them. I guess in the olden times people that were disciples were compared to slaves because of the loyalty and the need for them to be available for the trainers every beck and call. But Jesus let his disciples know that He did not consider them slaves but friends because He shared everything, He had hear from the heavenly father with them. In other words when God spoke to Jesus, he could have called it secrets and never let his friends in on anything, but Jesus chooses to share with his friends. He chooses his friends carefully, wisely and cautiously. He knew that birds of a feather flock together and so when you let people get close to you, you don't always know what they are capable of, but you got to be able to trust them. Even when they betray you, you have got to be able to forgive them and give them another chance friendship cost you something if it ain't nothing more than time invested.

It costs to be a disciple. A disciple had to spend time reading and studying and listening and doing and going and defending and watching and praying, spending time away from his family it cost dearly to be a true disciple of the Gospel. But Jesus said through all that sacrifice there was no greater love than a man to lay down his life for a friend.

I was watching out the window today and I saw y'all out on the playground. I saw Albert have his asthma attack I saw y'all as you carried him home and I noticed y'all spent a great amount of time in his house and even a greater amount of time on the steps just thinking." Big mama always amazed me how did she know we were sitting there thinking. "I couldn't help but think just what good disciples' you children were today. You could have let Albert's mother take him home and kept right on playing. I've seen others do him that way. But, you children, cared about him like a real friend. Well, I think that was pleasing to God and I think that if Jesus were around in the flesh, he would be glad to hang out with you three. You know the Golden rule says do unto others as you would have them do unto you. The word of God also says that you will reap whatever you sow. So, if you show kindness and thoughtfulness and friendship, it will come back to you.

What I really want you children to understand is, that true friendship is a gift from God. I believe that God knows we can't make it through life by ourselves, and that having someone there with you to share your good and bad times with is necessary for a healthy, wealthy life. Wealth is not always equal with how much money you have but how much good you've sown cause in the end the harvest is in the manifestation of heavenly treasures." Then that heavenly beam spread across her face. It always did, when big mama had heaven and God's will in mind. She asked, "Do you children understand?" I shook my head yes, but James and Jasmine shook their heads no. Big mama just smiled and said, "Well don't fret y'all understand it better by and by."

I guess we must have understood because for the next couple of weeks we keep Albert in our everyday activities. James and I stopped by the library every day after school, it was our daily ritual. Some days Jasmine would come, some days she wouldn't but for James and me, it was like we had to have a book every day. Besides they had just let black children have a library card. Even though the librarian thought it was best we leave it with her. Every day she would let us look at it as we checked out books. We were very proud because we had a card with our names on it.

James wanted to go to the hard books and pick out a book for Albert. After fumbling and thumbing through book after book, James finally chose one **OLD YELLER** a book about a dog. I laughed till I cried. James said, "He who laughs last laughs best now you watch and see if he doesn't like this book." "Well, the best and only one way to find out let's take it to him." I said shaking my head no. As usual, we both went home, changed our clothes and met on the old school yard before going to Albert's house. Today Jasmine couldn't come with us, her mother took her downtown after school. So, two of the three musketeers went to Albert's. He and his mother were in his living room watching television. They both looked up and shout "come in" together as James and I propped open the screen door, James said, "after you." "Good to see you," said Albert "I was just thinking about you three. Where is Jasmine?" He asked. "She couldn't make it!" We replied together. "We'll y'all need to stop sounding like parrots!" he jokingly replied. We all laughed.

"I found you a book at the library." James said, handing the book to Albert. "What? I don't believe it I just told my mother I wish I could have a dog. I don't believe this." He said smiling and teary eyed. James laughed and told Albert that he had told me it was the book that would make him smile. James laughed and said the Holy Ghost helped him pick it out. "Well why didn't you tell me that you were being lead. I almost screamed. "Then I wouldn't have laughed like Sarah." Then we all three laughed because it was a Bible story, we all were familiar with.

We had a great time that day, Albert read the **Our Daily Bread**, we prayed and played church. Albert was the Deacon; James was the preacher, and I was the Hallelujah lady. But we were careful not to mock the spirit because all the old folks told us that if we played with God, he would strike us down, so we were real careful and we were reading real scriptures and were praying real prayers and feeling real unction's. As a matter of fact, Albert said he was ready to meet Jesus and that he wasn't afraid of dying because he knew he would be with the Lord. Me, I won't be ready to go that far but I do believe I wasn't afraid. James well I don't ever believe I had seen him like that before not even in real church. He took his part to heart, and he just keep saying "have mercy on us **Lord Have Mercy!"**

He asked Albert did he want to be baptized in Jesus' name and Albert said, "yes preacher man baptize me." Well, I thought James had lost his mind when he took his glass of water in one hand and said to Albert. "Do you believe that Jesus died for your sins rose from the dead and waits for you in heaven?" And Albert said, "I do." "Then I baptize you in the Name of Jesus" and he poured his glass of water over James' face right on the bare floor. Well, I was supposed to say Hallelujah but instead I said, "AH!! James you're going to get in trouble." But them two wasn't paying me any attention they were shouting and dancing all over the floor, so I joined, and we shouted a while. We must have really been filled with the spirit because Albert's mother never stopped us, and Albert never had an asthma attack, and he really shouted up a storm. When we had finished, Mrs. Brownlow gave us cake and sent us on our way.

At the bottom of Albert's yard, James broke down in tears and ran back to Albert's house leaving me standing, wondering and waiting. I couldn't see anything but after a while Albert and James appeared with arms locked over each other's shoulders. Finally, they hugged, and

James ran back down the yard to meet me. "Are you all, right?" I asked. "Yeah." James replied. "Well, what was that all about?" I asked. "It's a man thing!" He replied. "Oh Yeah!" I sniggled. "Well, I guess I'll understand it better by and by." I said as we separated and went to our individual houses.

It was just two weeks left to practice for the Tom Thumb weddings and my great grandma Sallie Lou was making the costumes for the weddings. In Bluefield if you wanted an excellent seamstress, you employed my great-grandmother, she was the greatest. She had measured and fitted every child. She had Mrs. Aggie, another good seamstress working with her on the project and they were laughing and nipping and sewing their behinds off. She was in the middle of telling Mrs. Aggie that I was one of the queens when she stopped and told me that it was time for me to head down to practice. I never noticed her look at the clock, so I wondered how she knew what time it was. She told me that my sweetie pie was whistling in the street. I knew she was talking about James. I wonder how he knew I was up here. I kissed her on the cheek, hugged Mrs. Aggie's neck and hurried down the hill to meet James.

"How did you know I was up here?" I asked him. "Well when you didn't come down the street, I went to your house to pick you up and your big mama told me that you were at 123 Vine Street." "I knew it was right behind the church anyway and I needed to talk to you about something important before we went to practice." "We'll let's sit on the wall." I said pointing to the wall of the church where we were to go practice in. It was the wall I always saw teenagers sitting on at night whenever I stayed at Sallie Lou's and trust me it was never that often. She didn't like me like that. Clemmy was her mother, and they didn't get along good, and she thought I was just like Clemmy, so she didn't have a lot of use for me.

So, James and I sat on the wall and he started to talk. He told me that his father wanted to buy another house. The house was on another side of town. If his father bought it, then he would have to go to another school. He told me he was scared and that he couldn't tell anybody but me because he wasn't supposed to know anything about it. He was supposed to be sleep last night when he heard his mother and father talking. "Wow what a pickle you have gotten yourself into." I sighed. "But I know how it is though because I heard something one time, I couldn't tell anyone about either. But to tell you the truth right now I didn't know what to say." So, he said. "We had better keep this our secret." "Yeah, I agree. When it happened to me, I just kept it my secret." "Well now that I told you my secret and if we are best friends and soon to be husband and wife tell me yours." He insisted.

"Okay! Well, I overheard my mama and big mama talking about how Mrs. Walker said she had found some white people to buy me some glasses and my mother said she was not going to take me to the white neighborhood to get them. She said she was not accepting charity she would get her own money and buy me glasses and big mama says I could be blind first." "Really! Now that's a dill pickle. So, what did you do, did you tell your big mama you know she is really wise, Godly woman. My father said she was one of the wisest women he had ever met, and you know my father is real smart." James said confidently. He always smiled when he talked about his father.

"Don't be stupid, didn't I just tell you I wasn't supposed to hear grown folks talking? I couldn't tell my big mama she would know I was sinning by stealing into other people's conversations. It's our secret." I must have caught him off guard because he looked hurt. "I ain't stupid," he said, "I was just trying to help that's what a good man would do for his best friend." So, I apologized. "Listen I'm sorry please forgive me count it to me head and not to my heart." I always said that when I really meant I was sorry all other apologies were I'm sorry and James knew that we knew each other inside and out. "Apology accepted." He replied. "But let me tell you what I did, and I know it will work." James was curious now. "I went to church repented and prayed. I asked God to forgive me for listening to other people's conversations and to keep me seeing until my mother was able to get me some glasses. God did it for me in a strange way. He made it so that Mrs. Walker convinced my mother to take me to get glasses one day after school and she went with my mother and me. Mrs. Walker and my mother became good friends even to this day."

"Sounds like a plan I could work other than asking God to forgive me for ease dropping how should I pray? My father really wants us to have a bigger house, but I don't want to leave you and my classmates." James was so sweet. I was about to tell him what I thought when Sallie Lou hollering out the window and said, "You two are late for practice now get to get'n it."

We hopped off the wall and ran down the path that leads to the front of the church. Sure, enough, we were late. Mrs. Adams was putting people in their positions. She hadn't gotten to our group, so James and I slipped in quietly while her back was turned. Mrs. Cotton nodded to us and smiled, and we nodded and smiled back at her. Albert was at practice, and he was standing up front with his chosen bride. He was much taller than she and cuter I sniggled as I thought about him bending way down to kiss her.

Mrs. Adams turned around and looked at me, I was grinning quietly to myself. "Well, well if you aren't always giggling and cutting up, then you are late and unruly. I have half a mind to give your spot to somebody else. Now you get up there and find your position." As I walked to the front, I thought yeah, she got half a mind all right always picking on me. I have never done anything to that lady. I wish I knew why she didn't like me but then I remembered what big mama said be careful about what you ask for because you might not always be able to handle it when it comes true. So, I strolled up front like the lady I was and took my position.

We practiced and we practiced Mrs. Adams raised her voice at people all evening and she made people do things over and over again. Finally, Albert must have not been able to take it any longer because he began to breathe funny. James and I heard him when he asked to sit down and I believe in my heart Mrs. Adams did too, but she ignored him.

When I looked around Albert was slumping to the floor. I looked for his mother and she was not in the pews where she usually was. James was quick as a flash. He helped Albert to a seat and told me to find his coat that I might find the spray can. I almost knocked Mrs. Adams down as I ran to the spot where Albert had been, sitting and searched for his coat. I found it and true enough his spray can was inside his jacket pocket. I ran back past Mrs. Adams and to the front were James, Jasmine and Mrs. Cotton were now sitting. I handed the spray can to Albert and he breathed it in and laid his head back. It became quite noisy, and Mrs. Adams kept screaming for everyone to be quiet. Albert's mother rushed to the front where Albert was sitting and stooped in front of him and gently rubbed his head. Mrs. Brownlow was just such a loving, caring, and gentle, soft-spoken mother and a wonderful person. A blind man could see how much she loved her Albert. Once he regained his composure. Mrs. Adams asked him did he think he was able to continue in his role. Albert said he didn't want to. If she doesn't mind, please find someone else to take his place and then he asks his mother if they could go home. Mrs. Brownlow looked at Albert and asked him was he sure and he shook his head yes. So, she said she would call a cab. Mrs. Cotton told her to stay put she would call the cab for her and have someone come in and get them when the cab arrived.

Mrs. Adams went about the business of restoring order in her precious practice. The cab arrived, and we watched as Albert was being carried out, of the chapel by the deacons of the church. Mrs. Adams quickly chose a replacement for Albert and then to my surprise told Jasmine to take my place. Her reason was that I had disrespected her by trying to knock her down when I went to find Albert's spray can. She announced to everyone "That my behavior was atrocious. I had deliberately tried to knock her down and went into someone's personal possessions without permission. That she would not tolerate anyone who had such blatant disregard for other people, and I would be lucky if she allowed me to continue in any role in the play." I looked at James, then I looked at Jasmine and noticed Mrs. Cotton was sitting with her mouth wide open. Then I started to cry. At first, I believed I cried because my feelings were hurt then I believe I cried because she embarrassed me in front of all of my friends and lastly, I believe I cried because she was unfair. For whatever reason I was crying I just kept crying. I cried until practice was over. Mrs. Adams told me I was taking Jasmine's place, which was the maid of honor. I wasn't taking any place as far as I was concerned today, I quit.

When practice was finally over our sisters came to pick us up and I cried on my sister's shoulder. James told them what had happened, and my sister wanted to go give Mrs. Adams a piece of her mind but James' sister talked her out of it. So, she decided to tell my mother when we got home. Once we got home mama was still at work. So, Tyra went in the living room to tell big mama and I went upstairs to go to bed. After a little while big mama appeared in the bedroom with some bean soup and told me I missed dinner. I didn't feel much like eating but I felt like crying and that is just what I did. I laid my head on my big mama, and I cried myself to sleep.

The next day was Saturday, and it was James' mother's turn to entertain. So that meant we finished our chores and went to James' house for the day. I didn't want to go so I asked big mama could I say with her. Momma didn't think it was such a good idea by now Tyra had told momma what had happened, and mama was gearing up to confront Mrs. Adams. I was feeling sick on my stomach, so I used that excuse to stay home. Momma went on with her plans, she gathered up Ladybug and told me if I felt better, I could walk down to James' house. I told her I would and said have fun. I went back upstairs to bed. I could hear big mama downstairs in the kitchen, but I didn't even feel like talking to her. I just wanted to roll up in a big old ball and hide.

I must have slept a long time. The sun was plenty high in the sky when I finally sat up in the bed. I smelled good smells coming from the kitchen and some voices too. So, I ran down stairs to take a peck. Big mama was sitting at the kitchen table picking string beans. So was James and Jasmine. "Boy, we thought you would never wake up." Said Jasmine. "Hello sleeping beauty!" James said with a big smile. "Come over here and hug my neck." Big mama said. I hugged her neck, and she kissed me on my forehead and started to prepare me some luncheon meat sandwiches.

"What are you two doing here? I thought the Saturday fest was at your house this week, James?" "It is but the three musketeers can't function well with just two." He said grinning from ear to ear. James always knew how to make a girl smile. "Besides we had to come and tell big mama what happened yesterday and find out what we needed to do about it." "Well, I don't want anybody to do anything about it. I just want to quit and be done with it." I said angrily.

"Come over her and pull up a chair," said big mama "and let me tell you children a story." Well, if it's one thing I lived for that was to hear big mama's stories and no matter how bad I might feel, a good story from her was the best medicine in the whole wide world. Just then there was a knock on the side door. "Would you mind getting that for me please, James?" Asked big mama. Like the gentleman he was, he answered the door.

It was Albert Brownlow. "May I come in?" he asked. "Certainly! Man, how do you feel?" Asked James. "I'm doing better today. Good afternoon Mrs. Hairston, I hope you don't mind me stopping by without an invitation, but I wanted to come and thank Camilla for saving my life yesterday. This is for you." He handed me a card and a fake rose. I had got to get back up the steps my mother is waiting for me" he said shyly. "Thank you." I said grinning from ear to ear as I took the flower and card. "Please ask her can you stay; big mama was about to tell us a story." I said with excitement. "Yeah," said Jasmine "you don't want to miss one of her stories." So, he stepped out the door and asked her if he could stay for a while and James peeked out the door and told her that the three musketeers would make sure he got home. I could her he laughing as she told him yes he could stay and give her love to Rev. Hairston. "Pull up a chair baby and make yourself at home. Do you want something to drink?" Big mama asked. "Sure, that would be nice. Could I have some of the Kool-Aid you guys are drinking?" He asked. "Sure!" I replied as I got up to pour him a glass. I started to feel really special a rose, a card and three great friends and most importantly big mama sitting and sharing a story with me and my good friends, life can't be no better than this.

She started, "Back in the Old Testament of the Bible. There was a man named Jacob, and he was a man that had done some bad things in his time. He tricked his father. He stole his brother's birthright." "What's a birthright?" asked Jasmine. "A birthright is what the first-born son inherits when his father dies. It was the right to houses and land or valuables that amounted to double of any of the other children in the family. Well, Jacob's father was about to die, and he and his mother tricked his father into giving Jacob his brother's birthright because his father was going blind and he couldn't see too good. So, his mother dressed him up like his brother, made his arms hairy like his brother's and had his father bless him with something that didn't belong to him. When his brother found out he was ready to kill him he was very angry, so Jacob had to run for his life. He went to another country where his uncle Laban lived.

Now Laban had two daughters. His oldest daughter Leah wasn't as beautiful as his younger daughter Rachel, but Jacob fell in love with Rachel. So, he asked for her hand in marriage and Laban agreed and told him in order to get it he had to work seven years for her. Jacob did he toiled seven long years but because he loved her time went by real fast.

It was a custom of the country Laban lived in that the oldest daughter had to be married first so on the day of the wedding Laban dressed Leah up as the bride and wrapped up her face and body really good so that Jacob couldn't see her. He married Leah and the next morning Jacob realized that he had married Leah. Jacob screamed in anger because he had married the oldest sister and not Rachel. Well, I guess you can imagine how he felt. He was angry and ready to kill Laban. Sound familiar. Just let you know whatever you reap is what you sow. "Yeah," said Jasmine "Do unto others as you would have them do unto you." And we all chuckled. "Yeah, he was real mad." She continued. "He ran to Laban's house and got all up in his face and told him he was a lying, stinking, dirty, low down good for nothing scoundrel." We all laugh. "Takes one to know one!" interjected Albert. "Sure, you're right!" Said James and we all just cracked up. Big mama relaxed and continued. You could tell in her face just how much she was enjoying telling us Bible stories and I truly loved to hear them, so I said. "Go ahead big mama then what happened next."

"Well Laban told Jacob that in order for him to get Rachel as his wife he had to work another seven years for him. Jacob loved Rachel so much. He agreed. He worked another seven years and finally got Rachel to be his wife." Well to me it wasn't big mama's usual ending to a story.

"Well, what does it all mean big mama?" I asked, "I got the part about doing bad things and bad things happening to you and I also got the part about working for what you want but what else. "Well, I let you children put your own little meaning to the story. I'm sure if you four get together and talk about the story over playtime. I'm sure it will have an earthly meaning to you. So why don't you children just go outside and play before it is time for everybody to go home for the evening. Y'all go ahead and walk Albert home." Jasmine, and James looked as confused as I did but Albert, he was glowing like he had just seen God. Big mama, she just, leaned back in her chair and smiled. We all thanked her for the story and started out the door to Albert's house.

I can't even begin to explain how I felt. If there ever was a time that I needed big mama to come through with a solution now was the time, but she left me hanging. What did she mean by figuring it out on our own? Everyone looked dumbfounded except Albert, maybe he had a solution. As we walked up the tall, long steps of our front to the street that lead to Albert's house everyone was quiet. Albert still had a grin on his face. I was curious to know just what he was thinking but how was I going to ask him when he had no idea what had happened at practice after he left and I for one wasn't going to bring up that sore subject.

We had gotten just a little way off the steps and just in front of the shoemaker tree when Albert started to talk. "Hey James, have you ever climbed that tree?" He asked. "Sure man, many times, it's easy, want to learn?" "Why not, what do I have to lose?" Replied Albert. "Just your breath" barked Jasmine. "Not today I don't feel much like rescuing you again today." Jasmine said, "Oh that's not nice" I interjected "if he wants to climb my tree, I think it is a good time to teach him only one catch. You've got to tell me what you're smiling about." I inquired "Not a problem. If y'all teach me to climb the tree, then I will let you in on my secret." Well, I know secrets were all Jasmine needed to hear to get her attention. She loved secrets and she loved to tell everybody's secret too and I guess that is why James and I never ever told her anything we didn't want told.

First, I climbed the tree and sat at the top then Jasmine joined me. James gave Albert a boost to get started and he was a natural climbed midway the tree before he stopped. James climbed up and sat beside him and we all smiled and laughed. "Camilla, I know what happened yesterday was not your fault and my morn and I think it was unfair."

"How did you know, you weren't there?" I said. "Telephone girl Mrs. Cotton called my mother after we got home and told her all about it and when she came to tuck me in, she told me all about it. It was unfair and I think you three ought to do something about it." Albert demandingly said. "We're kid's" said Jasmine "what can we do about it? I didn't like her making me take my friend's place either when I believe that Camilla did for you out of love and what any good person would do. But my mother told me that it was just a play and if anyone would take care of it, Mrs. Garnet would." Jasmine stopped and looked at me. "Will you still be my friend?" She asked me. "Sure, it's not your fault, and James, I don't blame you for taking a bride you didn't choose either." Jasmine, Albert and I laughed but James, he started to give me that look. "Well if it takes me seven more years to work for you, I'm willing." As I said he never ceased to amaze me.

"Seven years?" Said Albert "Man you don't have seven years. A famous man I read about said you have to seize the moment. Your moment in time is right here right now. If you want to really teach Mrs. Adams a lesson in fairness, then when wedding day comes you step up and marry the woman that you chose. Jasmine, you know you weren't his original pick, don't you?" She shook her head yes. "Then it shouldn't hurt your feelings if James marries Camilla." She shook her head no. "Well just how do you suppose we accomplish that?" Asked James. Oh, wow another big word. I thought to myself. I wasn't about to hurt my soon-to-be husband's feelings by asking him where he learned it but he sounded so distinguished. I had a big word too. James and I had a private game where we learned new words and used them in sentences when we were alone to act intelligent and to privately joke, about people who talked funny so we wouldn't hurt anybody's feelings.

Getting back to the subject. Albert said it was too late for costume changes and that we were still probably going to have original costumes. "So, when the wedding started, Jasmine and I would change places before Mrs. Adams could get a chance to say anything. We would have to show up late but just in time to get in place. Then when the pastor asked James if he takes the bride to be his wife. James reaches over and takes Camilla hand and says I do. That just ought to send Mrs. Adams running out the church."

We all laughed till I almost fell out the tree. Albert was always so creative, he had a great imagination and to him it all seemed so easy and so real, but would it work? Would we be able to pull such a trickster off? Well one thing for sure, every one of us was feeling it and truly we would understand it better by and by.

We all climbed down the tree and headed for Albert's house. Once inside, his mother had made a big dinner, and she asked us if we wanted to stay around to keep Albert some company and eat of course. We were all game. Albert had some board games to play so we picked monopoly and started to play as we waited for dinner to be put on the table. Mrs. Brownlow turned out to be a very good cook and it was a whole lot of food, so we came to the table and sat down. She asked Albert to bless the table, and he prayed up a storm, he thanked God for each and every one of his new friends and asked God to continue to bring us around him.

When he finished, he looked as though he wanted to cry, and I felt him, and I guess James did too because he told Albert that we would check on him every day and especially if he didn't come to school and that that was a promise. Now I knew one very special thing about James he kept his promises and if he included me in something he wanted me to promise too. So, I told him I would try to make it every day but that was only if my big mama didn't need me. He told me he understood that family came first and that if his mother ever needed him, he would ride a horse naked to get to her. We all burst out laughing. It was great to have a new friend, and we friends were never jealous of each other, and we shared really well we were just like family.

It was the day of the "Tom Thumb" wedding, and we dressed in our original costumes. James and I arrived late just as planned and we eased to our seats. Mrs. Adams gave us an ugly glare, but she dared not say anything in front of all them grownups. So, we just sat and waited for our Que. Big mama and Sallie Lou and my mother were all there and so was my sisters and brothers. People we snapping pictures left and right as the children strolled down the aisles to get hitched. I smiled the widest smile I could smile as I came down the aisle in my wedding dress and Jasmine, she winked and smiled at me too as I strolled past the second-choice bride. When we got to the altar

James turned to receive his bride and Jasmine came down the aisle just glowing. The Pastor turned to James to ask him if he wanted to take Jasmine as his wife. He said, "No Sir, I chose Camilla and that is who I want to marry!" So, Jasmine stepped back and I stepped up to the bride's spot and held his hand. The whole church started clapping and laughing and some were crying. I wish I could have seen Mrs. Adams' face right then, but I was in tears myself. SO! The Pastor pronounced James and I, husband and wife. Then it happened James reached over and kissed me dead in the mouth. Then he grabbed my hand, and we walked proudly out of the chapel.

We didn't wait around to see Mrs. Adams, we all just ran out the church when the weddings were over, and people were talking about this being the best wedding they had ever been to. Everyone started to walk home, James' mom and dad, my mother and the rest of the grownups walked slowly behind us. Grandma and Grandpa Newsome brought big mama home in their car and James asked me if I wanted to be his real girlfriend. We laughed and joked all the way home, it was a great day.

Saturday morning was upon us once again and today seemed really different. I was anxious to get my chores done to get to Saturday fest today and to see my new husband, James. I just grinned when I said his name. I couldn't wait to tell big mama what he asked me on the way home. So, I hurried through the wash-up and put on my good holy clothes and hurried down the steps.

Again, there was nobody in the house, so I rushed outside to find everyone. There was a crowd of people standing in the street and there were red lights flashing bright and furiously. I felt a panic in my spirit. I never knew what a panic in your spirit was like before but today I am sure I had it. As I worked my way to the street and through the crowd I saw my big mama on Albert Brownlow's porch with his mother crying in her arms. The paramedics were inside, and they were from what I could understand working on Albert. I heard people talking and saying that he had had a severe asthma attack, and he might not make it through. Well just the very thought of him not making it through made me sick to my stomach and I wasn't going to let nobody see me cry cause they may not be able to understand what

I was feeling so I ran back to my house. Huffing and puffing I went to my corner of the couch behind the potbelly stove and fell on my knees to pray. I noticed my brother Vandy crouched in the corner as if he was in a deep conversation with the Lord. He called me over to him and we prayed together, and he was praying for Albert. I started to cry, and he held me real close and told me "Go ahead and cry I understand your tears." Then I boo-hoed as loud as I wanted because I knew, I was in good hands.

It was a good little while before big mama returned to the house and Vandie prayed all the time she was away. When she came through the door there was a peace upon her face. "How is he?" Vandie asked. "Well let's say that God has shined his light on him. They took him to the hospital." "Praise God!" We both said together. "Well where is momma?" I asked big mama. "She went to the hospital with Mrs. Brownlow, but she said to have you go down to James' mother's house and tell her that she was to have Saturday fest down there or cancel it for today. She'll be back as soon as she can." She sounded tired.

I got up from the couch and hurried along the way. When I reached James' house, he was on the front porch looking as if he had lost his best friend. "Did you see the ambulance?" he asked me. "Sure did, it was up at Albert's" I replied. "Well, someone told my mother that Albert died this morning!" He said. "What! No, that ain't true my big mama said the Lord shined his light on him." "Well, that ain't what I heard. My mother is in the house right now getting ready to go up to the hospital to see." He said sadly. I ran past him into his house and sought out his mother. She was in the kitchen. "Miss Anderson," I said, "I had a message for you from my mother but first is it true that Albert died?" "I'm not sure baby that is what people told me, but I got to go to the hospital to see for myself and to be by Mrs. Brownlow's' side." "Can James go to your house while I'm gone?" "Well, my mother sent me to tell you that she was going to the hospital too and that you were to have Saturday fest at your house or cancel it but sure James can go to my house, big mama is there." "Well thank her for me and I will get back as soon as I can." She said with her lovely voice that today sounded really worried.

I went to the porch and told James what his mother said, and we started up the street, it was a long walk today. Even though it was only a couple of houses away. James never said a word all the way to my house. But as soon as he saw my big mama, he burst into tears and fell on his knees in front of her on the floor. Vandie picked him up and carried him to the living room and when big mama sat down, Vandie placed him across her shoulder in the rocking chair. Then Vandie sat on the couch and beckoned me to come sit close beside him. Big mama started humming, "**Near the cross**" and tears came rolling down my cheeks. I looked over at my brother and he was crying too, then I knew what James had said about Albert was true. He had died. So I buried my face in my brother's side and cried. We cried until there were no more tears to cry and yet we were silent for what seemed to be an eternity. Then I began to wonder. Why did big mama lie to me? She had told me God shined on Albert, I thought it meant healed, brought favor or something like that not die. Well, I knew I would understand it better by and by but right then I knew as soon as it calmed down, I was going to ask about this light shining business.

It never seemed to calm down in our house the entire day. Turns out that Albert had a respiratory disease from birth that he had battled everyday of his life for the short time he was on earth. But big mama was bound and determined that Earth had no sorrow that heaven could not heal. James, Jasmine and I took it hard, and James looked like he hurt more than all of us so I was bound and determined to help him through this time if I could just understand it.

So when Big Mama finally found time for me. I sat down with her and began to think of serious questions to ask her. But before I could get the first question out. I had to make sure God was not striking us down for playing church a couple of weeks ago and so I told her the entire story. Turns out she already knew the story. Albert had told her the day after it happened when she went to his house to read *Our Daily Bread*. Turns out, Albert was teaching big mama to read and every morning before I even rolled over and farted, big mama was at Albert's house reading scriptures. He never went to school much and sometimes his mother would work a double shift at the hospital. So big mama would leave in the wee hours of the morning to sit with Albert after his aunt left for work and before his mother came in from work and returned before I even heard the alarm go off. Big mama would go to Albert's house on the days the teacher would come to home school him, and she would join in on the teaching sessions. It was all coming together like pieces to a puzzle. The only thing I couldn't understand was why big mama never asked us to go and play or visit with Albert. I guess she must have thought he was too sick or weak for friends. I wanted to ask her, but I remember that she told me something one time that some things are better left unsaid because what is meant to be will be.

I guess it was meant for us to be Albert's best friends, and it was meant for us to spend his last days with him, but was it meant for us to suffer his lost at such a very young age? Was it meant for Albert's mother to now be alone with her only child taken away? Was it meant for big mama to rock and moan in the middle of the night, when she thought nobody wasn't listening. She'd be crying out to the Lord to have Mercy and grant peace and every now and then weeping why Lord: but nevertheless, not my will be done but yours Lord. What was all this meant to do? Was it meant to strengthen my faith in God? Was it meant to help me look at life like a vapor and cherish every moment? Was God preparing me for something special in life that only I could do? I don't know right now but I bet I'll understand it better by and by. Even still it sure would be nice to have some help in understanding so while the blood was still running warm in my veins, I was determined to asked big mama to explain as much of this as she possibly could.

For the first time as long as I could remember big mama didn't want to talk. She asked me to steal away with her and pray but right now she didn't want to talk. So we slowly walked down the old school yard. She held my hand real tight like, kind of like a person that is scared and needed help. Could my big mama be scared? We walked down to the first church from our house and big mama turned the handle and went inside. I followed her up the steps and she went straight to the altar and anointed her head and my head with oil and lie before the Lord. I joined her on the kneeling bench. She prayed, wept and poured her soul out before the Lord and for the first time in my life I believe I saw GOD.

It was late in the evening and the sun was about to set in another hour or so. But the brightest light I had ever experienced was shining through the window and falling directly on my big mama. This was one of those times I was glad I listened to her when she told me you had to watch as well as pray cause if I had my eyes closed, I would have missed out. The light radiated down her head unto her back as the Holy Ghost had her speaking in tongue and screaming "YES LORD" in between phrases. I started to shake as she pulled me closer to her and the light fell on me too, but I wasn't afraid I said "YES LORD" too and closed my eyes as she laid her hands on my head and prayed. When I woke up it was dark outside and big mama was saying let's go baby. I looked at her and her hair was totally white. Her face shining like the sun and tears glistened in her eyes. Big mama was almost ninety and she got up off that floor like she was my age. I know we had been gone for hours and she had been praying all that time. Then she spoke strangely to me she said the mantle is pasted down to you and God's favor is upon your life walk worthy of your calling and give GOD your best daily. Well, I couldn't understand what all that meant but she did say you'll understand it better by and by.

Albert's funeral was at the funeral home and all of my family went. Vandy was a pallbearer and so was James older brother and Jasmines older brother. People cried hard and long and big mama read the scripture as well as gave remarks. She told the story that I thought was a secret that Albert taught her to read, and she said it as if she was truly proud of it and I believe she was. Then she started to cry as she told how much she already missed him and loved him. So, James, Jasmine and I cried some more. The preacher from Alberts church asked if anyone else had something to say. I was wiping my eyes and never noticed James get up. James stood up front in his three-piece suit looking like new money. He told the world what happened the day we played church at Albert's house. He even told me the part I had been waiting to hear. The part when he ran back to Albert's house. The Lord had told James to not leave his friend without hugging him and telling him how much he meant to him because he wasn't going to see him again. He told how Albert said we were the true friends he prayed and asked God for and if he never saw us again to remember that he loved and appreciated us and to never forget him. He told James that he would ask God to specially bless us when he got to heaven. Then James said I knew he was dying and the whole church broke down again. I think he was right too because Albert died the day after the Tom Thumb wedding caper he helped us pull off.

I was truly confused. I had known older people who had died in the neighborhood, and I also knew that heaven was a place prepared to receive God's saints. A place ever preacher I had ever heard preach talked about and every Holy Ghost filled person I had ever talked to spoke of one day having an eternally resting place. Albert, he believed in heaven and was looking forward to living with Jesus, so why was I, and everyone around me, so sad. I felt as though someone had taken a knife and jabbed me in the throat and my eyes were swollen and hurting. If heaven was what we lived to die for, then why is it so painful for all that remain and watch as the body goes into the ground. If I ever needed help in understanding something this was the big one! I needed to understand why a good kid like Albert would die so early. I needed to understand if God took children to heaven, did he have a special place for them or a mom and dad to look over them? I needed to understand this dying thing cause I was scared to death of it now.

James' father brought the house he had told me about. His father had a two-fold reason for staying on our side of town. First, because of the recent trauma that James had experienced his father decided he should finish out the year with good friends. Second, it was going to take some time to fix the new house the way he wanted it, so he was trying to buy time. James, Jasmine and me, well we were fighting sad times and trying to make good times.

We had to go and collect **OLD YELLER** to return it to the library so that we wouldn't lose our library privileges. Albert's mother really didn't want to let the book go back she said it was the last book he read but she understood.

Taking that book back was a hard task James, Jasmine and I wrestled with it all the way to the library trying to think of how we could keep the book. Then when we finally go there, we asked our now friend librarian what would happen if we lost a book. She told us that we would have to pay a fine of $1.00 it came from the children's book section. Even though it was from the hard back section, it was still considered children's books, so we went to the corner and discussed it. We decided to keep the book and pay the fine and we asked the librarian if she would help us with the math. We told her we needed to know what one dollar was divided into three ways was for each of us. She said it was thirty-three and a third cents each. We went back to the back and checked our pockets. We each had a quarter for candy and ice cream that we earned over this past week carrying groceries and doing chores. By now the librarian was suspicious and she came back to where we were and in that mean voice she used when we first got there, she asked us what we were up to.

We all looked at each other and no one said a word then she said again, "I asked you kids a question, now answer me before I take your library privileges away." Well, I for one loved the library and I wasn't going to let my card get revoked like my big mama said about voting rights, so I whispered a prayer and then spoke up. "Mrs. Gregory" I explained, "Our good friend died, and this was the last book he ever read. His mother looked really sad when we asked her for it back and so that we could return it so, the truth is we were going to lie and say it was lost. Just pay the fine so that we could give it to his mother, but we don't have a dollar between the three of us." Well, I guess even the toughest of the toughest can have a heart she told us she understood and told us to come with her. She told us to sit down in the seats out front. We sat for a long time and then she reappeared with three more **OLD YELLER** books, and she took the one James had and marked our card returned.

Then she asked us was Albert Brownlow the last one to read this book. We all shook our heads yes. Wondering how she knew. She wrote something in the book and said "Give this to his mother" as she gave the book back to me. "As for you three. You are special children. I want you to read what your friend read so here is a copy for each of you. Now get home before it gets late." "What about the f—Ine?" Inquired Jasmine but before she could get it out of her mouth, I had grabbed her by the hand and headed for the door. James, well you know, he had to be charming young man he was and stay behind thanking somebody all day.

Once outside we sat down on the sidewalk and opened our books. Each one had our names inside the cover. At the bottom was a note to the three musketeers that said, "Special and appreciated." Love Miss Gregory. "How did she know we call ourselves the three musketeers?" Jasmine asked. "You sure took a chance telling the truth about what we had planned to do with that book." James said smiling "Well," I said, "Big mama always say the truth will make you free and we got three free books!" We all laughed. "Besides I said you have not because you ask not, and big mama said as long as you are asking for a good reason then God don't turn you down too often. This was just a lot more than I had expected." So, we all breathed a sigh of relief and headed for Albert's house. With the first book I ever owned secure in my still trembling hand.

After changing clothes, we all met on the old school yard to take the book to Albert's mother. When we got to the spot that James made famous by running away from me and going back to Albert's house that last day we played with him, I started to feel something. It wasn't scary as a matter of fact; it was a friendly and warm sensation. I looked at James and he looked at me like he was feeling the same thing. So, we smiled our special smile at each other, looked up to heaven and waved. Then James reached over Jasmine and held my hand as we walked up the backyard. By the time we reached the front porch we both had tears streaming down our face and Jasmine stood silently in awe of what she may have been experiencing.

We knocked on the door and heard a pleasant "Come in the door is open." Jasmine almost knocked us down getting through the door and asking Mrs. Brownlow for a tissue. When she went to the kitchen to get it, Jasmine told us to wipe our faces she shouldn't see us like that. I don't know what she meant I felt good but when I looked at James he had tears on his face. I must have been in another world I had no idea I was crying. Mrs. Brownlow returned and told us to sit on the loveseat as we entered the living room. We presented Mrs. Brownlow with the book and told her what we had experienced at the library. She smiled and hugged us all and then she opened the book and read the inscription she began to cry, and we all rushed to hug her and comfort her.

She told us we were special children. Children with compassion and genuine love and that God had very special plans for each of us. He told us that Albert would be looking down from heaven and not to be afraid to talk about what we did not understand. I somehow knew that that was my clue to open my mind up to big mama so that she could help me understand death.

As we prepared to leave Mrs. Brownlow's house, she said she had a special gift for each of us. It was a toy from Albert's toy chest that he had picked out for each of us. Each of us got a GI Joe doll. I cried because I knew he loved his GI Joe's and he never let them go to war, they always worked for the Red Cross. I would often tease him when he and James played because James' men were always men of valor, rough and tough but Albert's men would always bring medicine and operate on the ones wounded in the war. He was just that kind of fella.

CHAPTER 11

Life's Raging Storms Require An Anchor!

Hebrews 6:7-19
Thus God, determining to show more abundantly to the
heirs of promise the immutability of His counsel, confirming it
by oath, that by two immutable things, in which it is impossible
for God to lie, we might have to lay hold of the hope set before
us. This hope we have as an anchor of the soul, both sure and
steadfast, and which enters thee Presence behind the veil.

The storms of life had just begun to rage in my life. There were not many days before school ended for the year and James and his family were excited about moving across town to their new home. The final assembly was about to take place at the school, and I was getting several school wide awards for reading and math. I wanted big mama to come, and she told me she wouldn't miss it for the world, but I knew in my heart she was weak, and maybe even too weak to come. Big Mama was getting older, and she didn't feel as energetic as she used to. As a matter of fact, she didn't even feel up to planting a garden when the spring rolled around so she put Vandy and me in charge of the vegetation and every now and then she would walk out and bless our garden. We seemed like a happy family, but it was a far cry from what I once knew as happy.

The final assembly came, and James and I were onstage together one final time. We both received awards for the most books read and best math students. James received an award for the most considerate student, and I got helper of the year. Grandpa and Grandma Newsome, my mother and Lorddybe. Big mama were sitting right up front when I turned to face the audience. She hadn't missed it for the world grinning and clapping and praising the Lord.

Big mama missed a lot of church as she was weakening so she sent me down the street to Sister Collie's house on Sunday to go to church with her. After church was over, the elderly ladies from the church would stop by and pray with her and serve her communion. I would sit and watch as so many of them cried and prayed to the Lord. It was becoming quite scary to me. Momma she had all but quit her job. She was afraid to leave big mama home alone most of the time in case she got too sick to cry for help. She fussed at her a lot telling her she was not willing to sit and see her waste away and then she'd leave in anger and sometimes in frustration of her helplessness.

One evening in the fall I came home from school to find my mother in the living room on the couch crying her eyes out into a pillow so that no one could hear her. I kneeled quietly beside her and asked her what the matter was. She sat up and pulled me close to her and told me point blank she was afraid that big mama was going to leave her. She said that through the years the only one she could ever depend upon and truly trust was big mama she was her momma. Now it was possible that she would die, and she wouldn't know what to do. I knelt on my knees and held her waist as she wept in my arms. I pat her long flowing hair ever so gently and promised her that it would be all right that God would make a way. He was a promise keeper and big mama said that whether we lived or died we belonged to the Lord. She boohooed! I wondered if she was crying so loud, why had big mama not come downstairs as she usually did when she heard someone crying. I let her cry and then I took my t-shirt and gently wiped her eyes and face and told her I would leave her alone while she pulled herself together. She kissed my cheek and told me she loved me. I got up off my knees and headed upstairs.

Big mama was lying on the bed reading her word and rocking from side to side. I asked her could I join her, and she told me that she preferred that I helped her into her rocking chair. So, I grabbed her under her arm and helped her off the bed. I was amazed at how much lighter she felt from just last week. She had had Grandpa Newsome build me my own rocking chair which was on the other side of the room so when I had got her into hers, I pulled up mine and we started to rock a while. After about ten minutes of silence, I asked her what she was thinking. "Well little lady if you must know and I know you must. I was thinking what a beautiful young lady you have grown to become. I was thinking how if I leave this world, I believe you and your mother will be the ones I miss the most. Don't get me wrong I will miss everyone, and I love Jesus, and I want to be with him, but I love this family and want to stay. Tears started to fly from her eyes. But you have to understand to everything and everyone there is a time and a season. A time to live and a time to die, a time to rejoice and a time to be sad but you never know when your season begins and for that matter sometimes when it ends. Sometimes you get a mixture of both. Sometimes you can't tell the winter from the summer. That's when I believe God steps in and gives you a measure of faith. A new strength that helps you stand in the times of trouble, laugh when things get funny, pray harder when you ain't got no money and trust in him much deeper when there ain't nobody to lean on."

"Baby girl, hear me good! I stopped rocking because when big mama said that I knew it was something I had to remember to survive. Life is funny, many people cross your path as you journey through life, some good and some bad. But the key to knowing who to trust and who to shun is praying and asking God for wisdom and direction. Then you have to make sound choices, that inside voice has to speak to you louder than the world that's crying out to you. It's a big world and trouble is everywhere, you can't run from it, you got to deal with the root of it in order to become an over comer.

Now take for instance this family God has blessed us exceedingly and abundantly above what we could ever ask or think. Now just don't look at material things, they don't have no value in the spiritual world. We have a long line of overcomers. My father and mother were slaves, and they did whatever they could to keep my family together. They sent messages near and far to my sister and brothers that were separated from us and they worked hard all day and provided for us at night. Even in the mist of troubled times, we prayed and believed God to see each other again.

What I'm trying to say is family is the most valuable asset you will ever own. Losing someone to death cuts like a knife but they are never dead as long as you keep their memory alive. Remember the special times, play them over and over again like you play a record." She looked at me and tried to chuckle. I knew what she meant so tried to chuckle too, but I was scared to death, and I was trying to be the big girl she had said I was, so I held back my tears for her sake.

She continued, after a long sigh, which sounded like a gasping for air. "People can never be replaced like some piece of furniture. Everybody leaves a mark in this world on somebody. I believe that I have helped mark you. Loving, caring, giving and knowing how to receive graciously is a lesson in life we all need to learn. Nobody doesn't have to do nothing nice for you and you ain't got to do nothing nice for nobody. But when you love the Lord and follow his commandments, it's an automatic reflex. Natural concern is what this world needs. The world could use more people who don't have a problem sacrificing the added luxuries to help someone else meet a basic need. Life really ain't about you and what you can get its about what you can give because in the long run you earn much more than you could ever give out when you put God's plan and His people first. It's the greatest feeling in the world to see a child like you grow and find the Lord. She turned looked me in the face and asked me "Have you found him yet?"

My momma was standing in the door now she had gotten herself together and made big mama a bowl of potato soup. She told me it was time I headed downstairs to join the others to eat. I wanted to stay and make sure big mama ate. I know she knew what I was thinking. So, before I could say it momma said "I will stay and feed big mama so I can get a chance to talk to her you done hogged up enough of her time as it is. Now scat!" she said grinning and winking at me. I stood up and kissed big mama and told her I would be back after dinner. She said make sure the table was blessed before we ate.

Everyone was at the table waiting for me. It was so quiet you could hear a pin drop on carpet. Vandy blessed the table and picked at his food. The soup was great, and the chicken was fried to perfection, but nobody seemed to have much of an appetite, but my knuckle headed brother. We ate slow and quietly. When we finished there was still food left over so knuckle head asked for seconds, Vandy said chicken yes, soup no that was for big mama.

Tyra went upstairs to her room to finish her homework and Vandy asked me did I want to join him in the kitchen to wash dishes and made knucklehead take out the trash. I agreed and we sang as we washed dishes, put up the food and cleaned off the table. Momma was still upstairs with big mama. When we had finished, we noticed that knucklehead still had not returned from putting out the trash, so Vandy leaned out the screen door that lead to the side porch and called out his name. He never answered.

It was time for us to get ready for bed, so Vandy carried Ladybug upstairs and I followed. When we reached the top of the stairs Tyra, momma and big mama were laughing and carrying on as if they were having a party. Vandy sure enough asked them why he wasn't invited then they told him it was a girl thing and then I asked them why I wasn't invited then they told me it was a woman thing, and I hadn't yet reached the age of majority. Whatever that meant? Well, I didn't understand it, but I knew one thing I would understand it better by and by.

Knucklehead had slipped away that night and got into trouble. Stole something that didn't belong to him again. This time the people wanted to press charges and because it wasn't his first time he had to go to court. Big mama was getting weaker, and momma was as well as could be expected.

Grandma Levy lived in Wisconsin and every May, she would come and stay for a couple of weeks and every September she would come and stay a month. This year wasn't any exception with the exception that she brought momma's sister and her children I had never met. Several of them could pass for white, they looked like Grandma Levy. I always wondered was she white and how she became momma's mother, but she was, and momma's sister she was close to white too.

Now one thing we were taught was to not be prejudice and make no differences, but I declare them people didn't look like they belonged in my family. But as soon as I got to hug my Aunt D and she hugged me I fell in love with her.

Aunt D was so funny. She had a very special way of telling a good story. She made every character have a different voice and she was kind too. They came by every day to see big mama, but they mostly stayed at Sallie Lou's house. She had nobody staying with her and she had a big house with plenty of room. Even though I had learned I had a bigger family it was still no consolation seeing that big mama wasn't getting any better. At the end of October, Grandma Levy and Aunt D were supposed to go home. I was wishing that big mama could feel better and really have a chance to enjoy her family, so I prayed double hard.

Around the first of October I came home from school to find the house locked up tight as a drum. After I checked all the doors, I saw Grandma Newsome peeking out the door. She told me she was supposed to look out for me. She said I needed to come over to her house. She told me that the ambulance had carried my big mama to the hospital and that everyone was up there. I felt a panic in my spirit the same type I felt the day Albert died. I wanted to go and run to the hospital. I knew the way it was right in front of my school. Why didn't somebody come across the street and get me? Grandma Newsome held me tight and told me she couldn't compare herself to my big mama, but she was my grandmother, and she had loved me from a distance all these years and she would always be there for me and that was a promise. I didn't know what she meant but it sounded good. She was a good person, and I believe she meant to look out for my good, so I held her hand as she led me into her house.

Nobody was there except she and I, so she led me to the family room with the piano and she asked me did I know how to play. "No," I replied, and she played a couple notes and said, "Name that tune?" We played the tune for a long time before Grandpa Newsome returned with my sisters and brother Vandy in tow. Grandma Newsome asked me to help her fix the table for dinner and we all sat down to eat at the big table in the big kitchen of Grandma and Grandpa Newsome's house. After dinner, Vandy, grandpa and Kevin Jr. (grandpa Newsome's grandson) went downstairs to play pool on the pool table Grandpa Newsome and his son Kevin Sr. built during the summer. Tyra, ladybug and I stayed upstairs and cleaned the kitchen then went to watch TV. It was getting late, and Johnnie Carson was about to come on, so Grandma Newsome told us we needed to get ready for bed. It was Thursday night and. ladybug and Tyra wanted to stay up and watch more TV. I wanted to go to bed so she led me upstairs to the guest room, turned down the sheets kissed and hugged me goodnight and left the room.

On the nightstand was a Bible and I prayed, opened it and started to read. It opened to **1 Thessalonians the 4th chapter**. These verses grabbed my attention. *I would not have you ignorant about those that sleep that they sorrow not, even as others which have no hope. For if we believe that Jesus died and rose again, even so them also which sleep in Jesus will God bring with him. For this we say unto you by the word of the Lord, that we, which are alive and remain unto the coming of the Lord, shall not prevent them, which sleep. For the Lord himself shall descend from heaven with a shout, with a voice of the archangel, and with the trumpet of God: and the dead in Christ shall rise first. Then we which are alive and remain shall be caught up together with them in the clouds, to meet the Lord in the air; and so shall we ever be with the Lord."* I closed the book, prayed for my family and went to sleep.

I had a dream that night, I dreamed I was standing on the balcony of a wonderful mansion and that I was really lonely. People were passing by me rushing from here to there and going nowhere fast. I was just standing and gazing up in the sky. I noticed nobody was speaking to each other as they passed. Children were fighting in the street and nobody tried to break them up as a matter of fact, nobody seemed to notice except Mr. Bo Skeet's, the wino. He didn't look drunk. I was on the balcony so I couldn't smell him to see if he was, but he didn't look to be drunk. He stopped and pulled the children apart and they ganged up on him. They were beating him something furious and I tried to scream but no sound came out my mouth. People keep rushing by as if they didn't even see the poor man getting beat. I looked up to the sky to pray for help and down came a cloud with my big mama on it. The light beamed like the day I was in church, and the sunrays almost blinded me. "Come on out of there! Time to come home" she yelled. I reached out my hand to her and she pulled me up on the cloud with her. I looked back and yelled for Mr. Bo Skeet's, and he broke free and ran towards me and I held out my hand and pulled him up. There on the same cloud was all my family everybody! My cousins from the patch, my aunt D and her family, my mother even, my knuckle headed brother was there and we all laughed and sang songs. We sang the song about putting on shoes and walking all over God's heaven and the song about walking with the king we sang a while. We floated on that cloud a good time then Ladybug woke me up telling me to move over so she could get in the bed. I couldn't get that dream back no matter how hard I tried.

But I dreamed another dream that night, it was a nightmare. Big mama died. I woke up the next morning sweating and screaming like a pig headed for the slaughterhouse. Momma apparently never came back from the hospital because we spent the night at Grandma and Grandpa Newsome's. momma had called and gave Grandma Newsome instructions on what she wanted Vandy and Tyra to do with us little ones and that was to take us out to Sallie Lou's house.

Now to tell you the truth I would have much rather stayed with Grandma Newsome. Sallie wasn't too fond of me. She always seemed to make a difference with me when she had other children around. Like she would make me wait for sweet cornbread while she passed out hunks to everybody then she would give me a much smaller piece like I didn't notice. The only thing I could look forward to was the fact Grandma Levy wasn't going to let her slight me. She stood up for anyone that somebody tried to do wrong. Even if it meant telling her mother she was wrong.

After breakfast we headed to Sallie Lou's house. Vandy walked us slowly. He looked like a robot not talking but looking straight ahead. I knew he was worried.

It was quite early, probably much earlier than I had been accustomed to getting out of bed but I knew it was school time and sometimes it was dark when we got out of bed. When we got to Sally's house, she feed us breakfast and told us we could go to school if we wanted too. Nobody ever gave us a choice about school. I always wanted to and today was no exception, so I elected to go to school. This year was really hard for me, James had moved, Jasmine wasn't in my class any longer and I hadn't really made any new friends.

It was always understood that if you left from a house, you returned to that same house when school was finished. So that was something I didn't need to be told but Sallie wanted me to know that since I was the only brave solider going out to school that morning I was to return to her house. Sallie Lou lived closer to the school than we did so I walked down to the crossing guard Mrs. Engle, and she smiled and asked how my big mama was. I told her I didn't rightly know but to keep her in prayer. She promised me she would. As she crossed me over to the other side, I began to wonder how I was going to get into the hospital. I knew they didn't allow children to visit, I had heard that over and over again, so I needed a good plan.

As I walked up the street planning in my mind how I was going to do it, Dracula and her crew pulled up on me. She was mean and ornery always looking to pick a fight, today was no different. She asked me where I thought I was going. I told her same place she was going to hell if I didn't live right. "Oh, you trying to be a smart aleck are you let me give you a quick lesson on respect." As she raised her hand to hit me. I said, "I don't need any lessons on respect. Respect is earned and you ain't earned a thing with me. Now hit me if you want to cause you got to bring a—", but before I could get the words out of my mouth, I saw a police officer walking out of the police station, and I ran straight towards him. I was really intending to tell him she was picking on me when he asked me was everything all right. I told him that I needed to get to the hospital to see my big mama and he walked me across the street into the hospital lobby. Once inside I told him I would be fine. I was told to wait right here until my mother returned. He wasn't buying it at first but then I sat down so I guess he believed I had instructions, so he left.

Once I made sure he was gone I walked over to the nurse's station and asked the woman if she knew what room Camilla Hairston was located. She looked at the register and back at me. She told me she was on a ward C but that I was too young to visit. I told her I understood, I just wanted to pray for that ward all day long while I was at school. She smiled and gave me a little more information. I don't understand why she did, but she did. She told me that ward C was right above us. Straight out that door in the back and up one flight of steps and to the right. If I was to go outside, I could look up one story and see ward C. I smiled and thanked her and hurried out the door. I knew that God was helping me form a plan I just hadn't put it all together yet. But I knew I would understand it better by and by.

School was just horrible. We went to the playground after lunch. William Mason and I had been friends from Head Start today we fought. What happened was that we had popsicles and when we finished, we were digging around in the dirt with the sticks. We spotted a bird that had fallen from a nest, and he was dying. I wanted to save it. William kicked it and killed it. I wanted to bury it, William wanted to leave it on the ground so the vultures could have a snack. I tried to move him so that I could pick the bird up with my Popsicle sticks and bury him, William shoved me. I don't know what came over me but before I knew it, I had hit him in the face several times and tore his T-shirt off of him. Next thing I knew, Mrs. Eveready, my third-grade teacher, was pulling me off him, as he lay on the ground covering his head.

Mrs. Eveready wasn't one for sending people to the office. She resolved matters in her classroom herself so she told me that she would think of a punishment for me when we returned to class. Dracula's class was on the playground too and she witnessed the fight. As we lined up to go back inside, she said something smart to me and I told her if she wasn't careful, I would beat the black off her too. Mrs. Eveready took me to the office. I wasn't in the office a hot second before Mrs. San Francisco wanted to paddle me. She didn't ask me my side, she never asked Mrs. Eveready what happened she just said bend over the desk I am going to give you one lick. Well, I wasn't bending over, and I wasn't going to do nothing until I had my right to speak.

"Mrs. San Francisco! You never heard my side of the story. I had good reason for what I did." I bellowed out. "Oh, you one of them smart talking Negro children," she said. Mrs. Eveready was turning red, and I was getting angry. "Well, call my momma" I said, "she never punishes us without at least hearing what we have to say." "Well, I am not your MOMMA! I said bend over this desk". She said with anger in her voice. I ran around the desk. Mrs. Eveready was in shock; she had never seen me act that way and I wondered did she ever have any idea that Mrs. San Francisco was prejudice? I don't know how we ever stopped chasing each other. But Mrs. Eveready grabbed me and told me she would take care of the matter as she hid me behind her. Mrs. San Francisco wasn't pleased; she wanted to throw me out on my head and slam the door behind me but Mrs. Eveready calmed things down. Mrs. Eveready had an assistant that was doing student teaching, she was a Negro so for the remainder of the day I had to sit in the back with her.

On Friday's we played a game called "poison". It was one of my favorite games. The object of the game was to find a seat where there was no book on the desk when the music stopped much like musical chairs. Mrs. Eveready wouldn't let me play and she wanted to talk to me after school was out.

After school, I explained everything to Mrs. Eveready. I told her all about the playground episode, about Dracula picking on me before school and my big mama in the hospital across the street. I asked her to forgive me for my behavior and she let me go with a hug and a kiss on the forehead. Miss Carr the assistant teacher asked me to wait for her. I stood at the door and waited, she seemed to be taking forever but once she was through, she asked me if I minded if she walked and talked with me. She told me she overheard what I was going through, and she wanted to help.

She took me across the street to the hospital, once inside she walked to the nurse's station and talked to the nurse. She gave her my big mama's name and the nurse told her where she could find her. It was a new nurse, at the station this evening, not the same one I saw that morning. I never forget a face and I had only been to the hospital one time, so I knew she was the nurse that was there the night of the

Pooch incident. Miss Carr grabbed my hand, and we started towards the door when the nurse said, "Sorry ma'am children are not allowed to visit patients." Miss Carr told me to wait right there, she would check on my big mama and she would be right back.

Well, she was gone for quite some time and when she returned, she looked as though she had seen a ghost. She told me that my big mama wasn't feeling well enough for long visits so I couldn't stay long. Then she did the strangest thing, she took me to the door that leads out of the hospital. She needed some fresh air, and she told me the plan. We were going to go back in and she would go to the nurse's station and keep the nurse occupied so that I could sneak up the stairs. Once upstairs, I was to turn right into the big blue room and go over three beds, there I would find my big mama. She made me promise that I wouldn't stay long and that I would be a big girl and not cry in front of my big mama so she wouldn't get upset. When I came back down the steps, she would be waiting in the hall by the big door that leads to upstairs. I agreed. She walked to the door and opened it wide; it was one of those doors that were slow to close. Then she hurried to the nurse's station and stood directly in front of the nurse. I all but crawled through the door quick as a flash.

Once upstairs, I peeked around the corner to make sure no grown-ups were in the hall and then I made my way to big mama. She must have been waiting for me because she had a glorious smile on her face. "If you ain't a sight for sore eyes," she said, "come here and hug my neck." I crawled up on the bed and hugged her, I hated to let go, but big mama was truly weak. She said, "I asked the Lord to let me see your smiling face one more time. God is good! She coughed and I could hear the rattling in her chest. Baby! Just always remember I love you. Remember your promises to me. That you will be a good person, teacher, writer, preacher, mother and all them other things you said. But mostly remember you are now the tie that binds this family together so be true to your calling, be strong and courageous."

I PROMISED! AND SHE CLOSED HER EYES AND WENT OFF TO SLEEP I HEARD HER BREATHE A SIGH OF RELIEF AND THE HALF-SMILE POSITIONED HER LIPS AS I KISSED HER FOREHEAD AND LEFT THE ROOM.

I sneaked back down the steps and there stood Miss Carr waiting for me. She told me to wait in the hall when she got to the nurse's station. I could sneak out and sit down then she would turn, and we could leave. As soon as she stood at the nurse's desk, I snuck through the door sat down and waited. She returned after saying excuse me then never mind to the nurse. Outside I thanked her for her help and then I burst in tears.

She let me cry as long as I needed to, so I sat on the wall in front of the hospital and cried. She held me in her arms and stroked my hair telling me it was all right; everything would be all right and it was all right to cry. But I knew in my soul nothing was going to be the same without big mama and I don't know if I really wanted to be all right without her. My spirit was filled with panic, my mind full of confusion and questions that I could not answer. Death seemed so cruel even though big mama said that it was so sweet to be with the Lord. That Heaven was where every believer looked forward to going from birth to the grave. I felt as if she had already left me and what was I going to do?

After I pulled myself together, Miss Carr walked me to Sallie Lou's house and offered to go in and explain why I was late coming in from school. I appreciated that and she also told me that the hospital visit would be our little secret because she could get into trouble for the rules. I promised her that I knew the difference between a good and a bad secret and I told her my loyalty would always run deep towards her.

Big mama said, sometimes people do things that don't always seem right but for good reason to help out someone else. I prayed that this was one of those times as I stood and listened to her explain the reason I was late, she didn't lie, and she didn't say that I was in trouble either. She simply said I had a lot in my heart and mind and that I needed to talk to someone that could help her understand what to do. Grandma Levy was a rational woman, and she understood and today so did Sallie Lou. Both of them looked worried and I could tell that Grandma Levy had been crying because her eyes were red as fire. Sally Lou must have been crying too because her nose was stopped up and she was breathing heavily.

Miss Carr was set to leave and Grandma Levy walked her to the front door. I was close behind the two of them and then I saw my brother Vandy, speeding like lightning to Sallie's house. When he got there, he fell at Grandma Levy's feet on the porch and burst into tears.

He cried and he cried, he looked like a six-foot rag doll sprawled out on the porch and he was so limp you needed a shovel to scoop him up. The grownups in the house ran outside when they heard him crying and no one even asked him what the problem was, it was as if his tears told a dreadful story. Grandma Levy leaned over the porch banisters and vomit and Aunt D started screaming. I had never seen Sallie Lou move that fast since my momma's accident. She didn't even reach for her walking stick, she just headed off the porch.

"Wait for me! I want to go!" Yelled Tyra. For some reason, no one even had to tell me where they were going. I knew they were going to the hospital. Grandma Levy finally finished vomiting. I ran and got her a towel and mouthwash to wash her mouth. She asked Miss Carr "If she didn't have any plans. Could she watch my sister Ladybug and me while they went to the hospital?" She didn't even have a chance to answer before Grandma Levy, Aunt D, her children, and some more people I had never seen before all rushed past me headed to the hospital. I tried to help Vandy up off the porch, but he shushed me away and grabbed the fence for strength to pull up. Then he took his T-shirt, wiped his eyes, kissed my cheek and said, "You be big mama's big girl and hold down the fort till we get back." He headed off the porch towards the hospital. As we stood quietly on the porch staring down the street. I knew what Vandy meant by holding down the fort, we always said that when we needed to fortify something with prayer. Then I heard my big mama's voice tell me "Do not be afraid, you will see me again someday just pray." I knew then without a shadow of a doubt it was time for me to steal away to pray.

As Miss Carr walked us back into the house, ladybug requested to lie on the couch so she could take a nap. I was truly glad because I needed time away and I didn't mean time to play. So I helped Miss Carr find ladybug's blanket and as she covered her, I told her I was going out back to cover my family. I raced to the back door of Sallie's house and stepped out the door in front of the chicken coops and started to talk to Jesus.

I first prayed that if there was anything that God found in me that was not pleasing to him to take it away, forgive me and make me aware so that I could correct it. Big mama said that was the way to clear the air so that God would truly hear your prayer. God knows I needed him to hear me today and I truly wouldn't mind if he spoke to me. So, I started pacing back and forth praying. I was beginning to feel warm and fuzzy inside and I must have begun to run out of words to say because all I could hear myself do was moan.

Miss Carr slipped out the door as if she understood and was in tune she began to pray. She prayed like my big mama. She would say a few words and then heave say a few more and heave some more. Big mama said it was the Holy Ghost speaking through a person and today I believed it more than I had ever before. Because she prayed what I had prayed and she never asked God to heal or bring big mama back but to comfort, strengthen and give wisdom to my family and me in the hour of need. She prayed with such sincerity and with so much power that I thought she must be praying for herself, no one could possibly care for someone they didn't know that well to pray for them the way she sent up the timber. I cried and for a second, I didn't want to be held by nobody but my big mama, but I could hear her voice saying she understands your tears lean on her. So as she reached for me I leaned upon her and cried a big wet spot in the front of her skirt as she finished her prayer and lead me back into the house.

It seemed like the hours crept by and it was getting dark. Miss Carr walked to the kitchen and found food that had already been cooked in the oven and side dishes in the refrigerator. She prepared her and me a plate; ladybug was still sleeping. So, we sat at the table, and I asked her had she ever known anyone to die? She told me she lost her grandmother right before she graduated from high school. Her grandmother was her best friend, and she shared a great deal of time listening, doing and caring for her grandmother. It was almost five years, and she hadn't gotten use to the fact that her grandmother was not around to talk to. It must still have been painful because her eyes were swollen with tears and just for a moment, I could feel her heart's pain because it felt like mine felt at that moment. So I cried some more and she cried with me. No sooner had we stopped crying and pulled ourselves together. Ladybug got up hungry and cranky.

It seemed like forever before anyone returned to finally confirm what I had already known. So, when my mother called me and ladybug together to give us the bad news they were shocked that I didn't break down and cry, but I was out of tears and I was ready to feel the joy of knowing she was finally truly happy. After all that is what she told me, she lived holy for so that when she died, she could go and live with Jesus. It was truly her reason for living the Godly and good life she lived. To show God that she appreciated the fact he allowed her to live. It didn't matter how much suffering she had to do, how many times she had to be a little hungry with just enough to survive in her stomach. It didn't matter that she wasn't able to buy cloth to make a new dress for church but once a year she was content in knowing God was pleased with her sacrifice, lifestyle and heart for others. Well, I knew God must have been happy because she once told me that God was happy with the death of his saints.

I on the other hand wasn't and I didn't believe I could be, I had lost my best friend, my guide, my storyteller, my precious big mama. What was I going to do? Just thinking of what I was going to do made my head hurt. Even though I wanted to cry, my heart began to become glad because I knew I could hold on to her words and that smile as she breathed a breath of air and went to sleep.

My secret visit was the last visit she had ever had according to the time momma said she died. I had just left the hospital with Miss Carr. According to momma, she had a glorious smile on her face and she was still warm when they got to the hospital. Well, I knew absolutely nothing about what that meant but I knew that if there was still blood running through my big mama's veins, she was praising the Lord even in her sleep. And that was sure to make a smile come on her face.

I understood that death was final for the people that lived here on this earth, but I also understood that **HEAVEN** was a place for prepared people to rest for eternity. I believed that Albert and big mama were probably in **HEAVEN** reading **OUR DAILY BREAD** book together and she was probably telling him a story. That's when I began to cry. Just thinking about her not being able to tell me no more stories and how now all the other children in heaven were going to have my big mama, to guide them, hug them, smile, and laugh with them. Secretly wink at them, help them, love them and tell them the stories I wanted and needed to hear. I believe that day I started to die inside and started looking forward to waking up in heaven with my big mama.

Nevertheless, I knew deep down in my heart, she had placed hope inside of me and given me a pathway to survival. So I had to live, I had to go forth for how else would I get to realize what big mama said that, "You will understand it better by and by."

CHAPTER 12

Are You A Covenant Keeper?

Jeremiah 31:31-34
Behold, the days come saith the Lord, that I will make a
new covenant with the house of Israel, and with the house of
Judah: Not according to the covenant that I made with their
fathers in the day I that took them by the hand to bring them
out of the land of Egypt; which my covenant they brake,
although I was an husband unto them, saith the Lord: But this
shall be the covenant that I will make with the house of Israel;
After those days, saith the Lord, I will put my law in their
inward parts, and write it in their hearts; and will be their God
and they shall be my people, And they shall teach no more every
man his neighbor, and every man his brother, saying Know the
Lord, for they shall all know me, from the least of them unto
the greatest of them, saith the Lord: for I will forgive their
iniquity, and I will remember their sin no more.

The days seemed so long and dreary, even though there was an innumerable amount of family arriving for big mama's funeral. People hugging and kissing, crying and laughing, it was just a mixture of emotions, and it wore me out. For instance, I might walk in the room, and they would be laughing and joking, and someone would call me over to them and ask me my nickname and I would say "Little

Clemmy" and someone would start crying. I was too scared to say anything, even though I did enjoy the love and attention. I missed my big mama's hugs. I knew I was spoiled rotten because nothing anyone could say or do would make the sick feeling in my stomach go away.

Finally, it was time for the funeral services. I was dressed like a princess, pretty new clothes, hair pressed to impress, shoes shining like a new dime, heart heavy and tears sliding off my Vaseline, greased down face. I could hardly stand up straight, my knees felt as if they would give out as I climbed into the back seat of the limousine. The ride was slow and as I looked out the window, I saw car upon car lined up and down Jones Street. As we turned the corner to Bland Street, I saw more cars lined up and when we arrived at the church there was nowhere to park because of all the cars that were there, so the driver stopped and let us out in front of the church. People were standing on the sidewalk quietly and respectably. Men had their hats in their hands and not on their heads. Big mama said that was a sign of respect when men tipped or took off their hats in the presence of a lady.

As we lined up to go into the church, I saw Pastor Blaine standing up front holding his Bible. "Hi Pastor Blaine!" I yelled. He turned around. Meanwhile my brother told me it was time to be quiet, I would be able to speak to him later. People were still lining up and Pastor Blaine had made his way over to me. "Praise the Lord little sister you certainly look like an angel today." He said smiling at me. "Thank you. But I don't feel much like one right now." I replied. "I understand your troubled child, but Rev. Hairston is now sleeping with the Lord and there is no better place for her to be now that her work is over here on earth, baby you might not understand it now, but you will understand it better by and by." Then he hugged me and walked back to the front of the line.

As we walked past the people, some crying, some holding back tears, some shaking and others smiling down at me, I felt loneliness for the first time in my life even though I was in a crowd of people. My knees shook with every step I took. My stomach bubbled and I knew I had enough to eat. And the tears, the tears wouldn't stop flowing down my face even though I told myself time and time again I won't cry, I won't cry, I know big mama is with Jesus I won't cry. It would just not work.

When I got inside, I couldn't see what was going on up front but one of Sallie's sister's children was screaming and crying and the deacons were dragging her to a chair. The ushers were fanning her. I looked again and they were dragging Sallie Lou to a chair. I was getting closer now and the anxiety in me was making me shake even the more. Then I was right up on the box covered and surrounded with gorgeous flowers. Vandy picked me up so that I could see and in that flowered covered box laid my big mama with that glorious smile on her face. That same smile I saw when I left her room at the hospital. It was as if she was smiling straight at me, so I smiled back and said to Vandy "Big mama is sleeping let's wake her up, I want to tell her something." I stretched out my hand to shake her shoulder and Vandy snatched my hand back and took me away to the next seat. I looked at him and he was crying. I put my arm around his waist, and he laid his head on mine and broke down.

Today I knew how Humpty-Dumpty felt when all the king's horses and all the king's men couldn't put humpty back together again. The walls of my life had collapsed. My big mama (my Nehemiah) had come down off the wall my brother Vandy who was a strong tower as now cowering in my arms soaking my head with tears. My family was falling down, getting up and falling down again. Me, I had to pee, and I had to go right now. So, I raised my hand and one of ushers came over to me. People were still coming in lining up around the walls of the church. I told the usher my dilemma and asked her to take care of my brother while I was gone. She picked his head up slid in my seat and laid his head on her shoulder as I slide from under him and raced past everyone standing in the corner by the bathroom door. I was praying it wasn't a line cause truly I couldn't wait. I must have said excuse me a thousand times or more. I opened the door, and it was empty, so I eased up my dress and climbed up to the toilet. It was cold and the room was cold, but it was quiet and peaceful. I wanted to stay there just a little while. I closed my eyes and just sat there. I leaned my head over to the cold washbasin and cupped it on my arm. It felt good to my hot skin. It was like a place you could escape to and maybe speak to God in private, it was a calming peaceful feeling that came over me. It was a place and time that I needed to speak to God and maybe if I listened closely, I could hear God speak back to me.

So, I started my conversation with God. "God, I don't know what to do or think who is going to take care of me now? Everybody says big mama spoiled me rotten and that I have a strong will just like her whatever that means, and I overheard the grownups say that unless you spoke to me, I would be lost. I also heard them say I might not be right in the head no more unless somebody explains what happens when you lose somebody you love, and nobody wanted to take that task on. God, I know I have been wrong for being a little pitcher with big ears but please forgive me and help me not to be so nosy. God what do I do now? Who do I talk to about big mama? Will anyone understand my tears, my fears, and my heart? God, please let a word come that will give me direction, show me that I am not forsaken, and that you really do have a plan for my life. I may be young, and I may not understand what happens next, but I am willing for you to teach me, and I promise I will obey, just speak Lord speak to me." I whispered. For a moment I thought I heard the Lord speaking, God said, "I will take care of you. Are you alright?"

Then the knock came, it was loud. I got afraid because I thought God was knocking on the door of my heart and I wasn't quite sure how to answer it. So, I sat quietly then I heard it again, it sounded as though it was coming from the door. "Are you alright in there." It was a person speaking from the other side. "Yes, I will be finished in a minute." I answered. "Okay put a rush on! The service is about to start, and we can't start it without you baby." I recognized the voice now it was Sister Collie. She always looked out for me. So, I finished my business and pulled myself together, washed my face with cold water just in case there might be tears and I opened the door. There she stood glowing and smiling and reaching out to hold my hand. "You know child, God's got something really special for you to do in this world and just as soon as He wants you to do it. He will have you prepared. Cause God always prepares us to do something and then He asks and then He expects you to do it. Do you understand?" "Not really!" I replied. "Well, you will understand it better by and by." she said. I smiled at her. From that moment on, I was comfortable with her for I knew she loved my big mama, and she loved me too, so I wanted and decided to stay by her side.

We walked back into the chapel and the choir was singing big mama's favorite song ***Rock of Ages***. I sat down by my brother, and he held my hand. He never spoke, just held my hand real tight. I could see big mama laying in the box smiling her half smile and looking as if she was at peace. Just listening to the choir sing. Then the choir got excited and sang the last verse "While I draw this fleeting breath, When my eyes shall close in death, When I rise to worlds unknown, and behold thee on thy throne Rock of Ages cleft for me let me hide myself in thee." I relaxed knowing full well that big mama was now with Jesus.

Pastor Blaine was under a heavy anointing. He spoke clearly, loud and commanding like. It was if he wanted to make sure no one went to sleep and that everyone heard what he had to say. His sermon was **"Are you a covenant keeper?"** A question he wanted us all to ask ourselves and answer. He said God had made a covenant with each of us that in order to be a part of this covenant, we had to first know and recognize who God is. He is not a man that He should lie, He is not a promise breaker, nor does He give us gifts and want them back when we don't do right. He is the creator of all things and knows us better than we know ourselves and yet He gives us mercy and undeserved favor. God is also holy and cannot look at unholiness and leave it unpunished because He is also a just God. Therefore, man has to recognize that he cannot save himself even if he did good works all his life. He would still have sin and need a savior. The only Savior was Jesus Christ the Lord and that no one could go to Heaven unless he first trusted Jesus to be the Lord of his life. Jesus was the gift giver and Salvation, and eternal life was wrapped up and tied up in him and unless we took the gift freely and accepted him and expected him to live inside of us, we couldn't be partakers of the covenant.

Secondly: In order to be proven a covenant keeper, fruits had to come out of you. Unless it was in you it wouldn't come out so the fruits would never show unless you first put them in you. Now I really started to wonder because I loved fruits, and I ate them all the time, but I never saw any of them come out of me. Maybe I wasn't a covenant keeper. I keep listening. I am talking about "Spiritual fruits." The fruits of the Spirit are love, joy, peace, long-suffering, gentleness, goodness, faith, meekness, temperance and if we live in the spirit, let us also walk in the Spirit because once we have the spirit inside then what's in you will come out. I felt a little better. Now all I needed to know was how do I get them or did I already have them. I needed a piece of paper so I could write them down and look them up in my new dictionary when I got home. But I knew better than to ask someone for something when the preacher was preaching. Big mama said there was a code of conduct in the house of God and respect was number one. Quietness and attention came in second on her list. I smiled to think of what things I remembered from being with her but right now I couldn't afford to let my mind wonder because I had to concentrate on the word and the fruits. So that I could meditate on them later when I got to my secret closet.

Pastor Blaine continued to talk about the covenant that God had made, he said that everyone would know God for himself and that we wouldn't need a teacher because God was going to write his covenant on the tablets of our hearts. He said God knew the family you would be born in. He knew the struggles in life you would face. He knew that someday faith would become real to you and that walking by faith and not by sight would be your daily struggle.

He said he didn't know about everybody, but he uses to sometimes wonder that if God was supposed to be so wonderful, and so kind, then why did he have to struggle daily? Bringing in wood and coal and carrying water from house to house when the pipes freeze and burst. Why did he have to work from sunup to sundown to put food on his family's table and stretch every dime robbing Peter to pay Paul? If God's word says cast all of our cares upon him for, he cares for us then how do we get his favor when we are already walking by faith, living holy, praying and doing everything we know how to do to stand?

He said, my children I tell you God knows, and he feels our every infirmity. He doesn't give us trials to kill us or make us cower in a corner, but He trusts us with the pain, and He trust us with the trial, and He tries us according to the faith we claim to have. Then he shows us how much strength, stamina, courage and obedience we have inside of us when He has tested us and like Job, we can say though He slay me yet will I trust him. Our trials make us not only physically, but also spiritually strong. For as we trust in the Lord with all our hearts and lean not unto our own understanding and all our ways acknowledge him. Then his direction of our paths whether it appears good or not at the time, will one day work together for the good of those who love the Lord and are called according to his purpose.

Because our God is Sovereign and He wills and does as it please him then because we know God wishes above all things that we prosper and be in good health even as our soul does prosper then God wants only good for us. He directs the steps of a righteous man. Not everything is instant, there is not always and easy fix but God wants to pull out the potential in all his children by allowing them to apply his word and see his magnificent way of making a way out of no way. God alone can get the glory when we see his hand move in places that we humanly cannot accomplish.

He has made a covenant with his people. He promised to bless us and supply our needs according to His riches in glory. No man will ever be as rich as God. He created and owned everything, and man is without excuse for not recognizing that the true and living God exists and lives today. Mankind was created for fellowship, friendship, and relationship. For we are the workmanship of God's hand, and God is the owner and captain of every ship that sails in the sea of belief. He will take what looks bad and work it for our good if we faint not and even if we faint if it be so in his plan it will come to pass.

The covenant that speaks to every man, woman, boy and girl says that we must know the Lord and that no man would have to teach anyone to surrender his life, mind, body and soul to the true and the living God Jesus Christ. Because inside of each of us is a God that cries out and knocks at the door of our heart saying seek me, find me, and worship me. Have you found him yet? Have you stopped grumbling and complaining about what you don't have long enough to see what you do have? If God is in you and for you then He is more than the whole world against you, if you believe and trust his word. Jesus didn't come to lay down his life to be of no effect but to affect the quality of life his children would live to provide hope, strength and courage for the journey and a secure eternity.

Today if you want to be a keeper of the covenant with the Lord Jesus Christ then ask yourself these questions. Am I willing to allow the spirit of the Living God to rest, rule and abide in my life, to direct me and protect me and comfort me as I become obedient to his voice? Am I willing to stand firmly on the word of God and no matter what struggles come my way never let go or compromise the standards of God's word even unto death?

Lastly, am I willing to decide right now and walk up to this altar and hand over my insecure life for eternal security? If you can answer yes to these questions then make that first step, walk to this altar and surrender your life to God so that He may bless you with eternal life, use your gifts and talents and give you strength and courage. He wants to give you boldness, riches of unspeakable joy in your soul, peace in your mind, love and forgiveness in your heart, and hope for your future that keeps dreams alive and memories flowing from generation to generation. If you want to experience God close and personal come now while God is troubling the waters of your heart and feel the touch of the Lord that will lift your spirits, comfort your mind and give you a boost that will make you never the same again. Come just as you are, and God's spirit will not allow you to stay as you are as He perfects his will through your life.

I had heard many altar calls. Big mama said it was the time in service that people made decisions as to whether they really wanted to walk in relationship with God or not. She said it was the most important time of the service and that I needed to be in intercessory prayer for souls as the altar call came forth. So, I always bowed my head and started to pray the prayer she taught me.

"Please God touch the souls you have prepared to hear your word to surrender to the Holy Ghost. To have the courage to walk to the altar and surrender to you their sins, that have separated them from your will for their lives. And please God as you look upon the true heart of every man, woman, boy and girl forgive their sins, cover and hedge them and their family in with angels, grace and mercy for the duration of their lives on this earth. Thank you, Lord, for your faithfulness to your undeserving people. AMEN."

I was praying my prayer, when I heard Pastor Blaine say that if trusting and believing the covenants of God was good enough for Rev. Camilla Hairston, a woman of great faith, courage and an example for us to live holy. Then it ought to be good enough for all of us who loved her and believed in her as a soldier in the Army of the Lord. I opened my eyes to see that he had stretched forth his hand in invitation as he always did but today it looked to me as if his hand was glowing and motioning me to come to the altar and so I did. I was the first one to the altar I used the hurry up motion. My brother, Vandy, followed me, and so did Sallie Lou, big mama's other daughter, and quite and few others.

But the story doesn't end there. I could see big mama's face so clearly; it will always be etched in my memory. I saw a tear slowly roll down her face while she slept in that box and a beam of light lifted from her to the ceiling and shined directly on my face as it departed through the roof. Then a tear streamed down my face on the same side as I smiled and placed my knees upon the altar. I heard her say, "I knew I could trust you to lead them." For the rest of the day, from the time we left church until the time the pallbearers laid her in the grave, I spoke not a word but cried softly yet uncontrollable on my brother's shoulder. When my brother realized that my mother was in trouble, he handed me to one of my uncles and raced to help my mother. I cried on him until we returned home. I couldn't stop crying.

As soon as we got in the house, Grandma Levy took all the girls upstairs to change our clothes and get ready to go outside. It must have been at least fifteen of us in one room changing clothes and everyone was talking to me, around me and maybe even about me because I wasn't talking back, just crying. But I couldn't stop crying long enough to focus on changing. I also knew that I couldn't ever tell anyone about the experience that I had at church that started my tears because I knew in my heart that my family as I saw them, were ready to go and get their drink and party on and they would never understand.

Big mama was the cord that upheld good and whipped up on evil. She single handedly went to battle against the devil in our house. She was bound and determined not to let Satan have a foothold because she said he was a greedy, selfish old devil that if you gave him an inch, he would take a mile, and I believed her because as I thought on her words it made me smile. Thinking about seeing her any hour of the day praying or meditating on the word and rebuking Satan at every turn made me feel better. Big mama never ceased to amaze me with the countless hours she spent on her knees interceding for people. She told me one time that when you get as old as she was, and she couldn't always go see about someone then she invoked the spirit of the living God to go for her. That God was never more than a prayer away and the effectual, fervent prayer of a righteous man availed much. In other words, living holy had its privileges with God.

I purposed in my heart that day, that come what might, I would stand on the promises of God and on the promises, I made to my big mama. That I would seek the Lord with all my heart and with all my soul and with everything within me until I found the true and living God and applied his word to my heart and life until Jesus returned for me to live with him in eternity. Now all I needed was directions on how to get it right. So, as I finished changing my clothes and between sobs, I asked Grandma Levy if I could stay upstairs for a while to get myself together. She quickly agreed and took the other children away so I could be alone.

I prayed as I had never prayed before. Jesus didn't just have his hand on me; He must have had his whole arm around me. There was a quiet peace, a feeling of joy, a sense of power and the presence and smell of big mama right in the room. The room I didn't leave from except to use the bathroom the next three days. I fasted and prayed for God's direction, and he sent Doctor Hickman to my rescue.

Nobody could have known what I was going through. I never told a soul, but my momma knew, and she wasn't going to let me go through by myself and get sick on her, so she called doctor Hickman and told him he needed to make a house call. He came and we talked, and we talked, and we talked some more. He told me that he knew God as a healer, deliverer, savior and guide and that he also knew that God wanted us to be healthy and strong. That if I went on a starvation diet, I wouldn't be doing what God wanted in his will for my life therefore I had to eat. He promised me that he would see to it that I got someone to carry me to church on Sunday if I was so adamant about going and he promised me that anytime I wanted to talk to him he would be available.

He kept his word and Pastor Blaine sent Mrs. Collie every Sunday to make sure I got to church, sometimes I just packed my bags and spent Saturday at her house, but I always went to church.

It wasn't long after everyone had returned to his or her homes and daily lives started to become normal again that all hell started to break forth in my family. Knucklehead had gotten into trouble and was sent to a boy's home for six months. Vandy had to face charges of assault against Pooch for beating him up for what he had done to me, and my friends. The judge told him he had to go to Job Corps unless he wanted to go to jail. So, they sent him to Portland, Oregon on the other side of the USA. My momma, she started drinking to calm her nerves and relieve her tension. To make matters worse, Mrs. Collie had gotten deathly ill. I had to go to church by myself, which meant I had to tell my momma a "little white lie" in order to get her to let me go because there was no one willing to take me and I hadn't asked anyone else to come and get me. I was afraid to ask, until one Sunday I heard Pastor Blaine say you have not because you ask not! So, I asked, and I received a new Bible and **Our Daily Bread** book to read daily until they could find someone to pick me up and bring me to church and I wouldn't have to lie any more. I waited Sunday and after Sunday and no one came then one day I heard Pastor Blaine had died and so had Mrs. Collie. It was as if they died back-to-back. I became numb with fear and questions that I had no one to ask and get Godly advice.

By now my house had become a den of sin and my faith was on the borderline of the grave and/or compromising to fit in. Where was I going and would there be anyone one who could lead me?

I realized at that moment in time that I had a crossroad decision to make. Big mama said those were the hardest types because not all roads lead to Christ. "Trouble would come from all ways but it didn't stay always." It was like her voice started to speak clearly in my ears. If I was to become a covenant keeper without a covering or a guide then it was up to me to seek it, find and live the covenant whether anyone came with me, or I had to go by myself. After all Pastor Blaine said, one day there would be no need for a teacher because they would know the Lord from the least to the greatest.

"Big Mama" had raised me in the way I should go. Taught me to observe all things, took me to the water brook and gave me a golden cup to dip from the fountain of life.

Pastor Blaine had armed me with the sword of Word of God to fight the fight of faith and endure like a good soldier.

Sister Collie had shown me what true friendship and loyalty to a friend meant. She displayed it in her care, compassion and faithfulness towards me after big mama died.

I had been through basic training. Today began the days of testing in my life and I prayed and studied God's word so that I would be well prepared for the tests that would come in the near future.

Man has a problem that places him in a predicament that he cannot possibly resolve in his finite humanity. He is a sinner in need of a savior. According to Romans 3:23 "All have sinned." Man is a sinner and no matter how much emphases he places on living holy and doing cannot stand to look upon sin and right he cannot save himself.

God is holy. God cannot stand to look upon sin and therefore sinful man is rightfully separated from God. The Bible tells us in Romans 6:23 that the "wages of sin" is death or separation from God for eternity. God is a just God and cannot allow sin to go unpunished however, God is also merciful and gracious. Always willing to reconcile with man.

Man has no excuse for the denial of the true of the living God because the heavens and earth declare his Glory in everything. God has supplied a way for man to enter into his eternal rest. Jesus sacrificed his life to free-heartedly pay a debt he didn't owe for us debtors who could not pay. Believing by faith, in the death, burial and resurrection of Jesus Christ, as our substitute for sin, we can be forgiven and given eternal life. Each individual man has a free will choose in which he needs to make, a crossroad decision that can only be made as we journey through this earthly life. For eternity is promised but where is a personal decision.

If you want to prove the existence and faithfulness of God pray this prayer. "Dear God, I believe in your son Jesus Christ. I believed that he was crucified, bled, died and buried for my sins. I believe that on the third day he rose again from the grave and now lives in heaven with God waiting for me. I want to be your child. Please God forgive me from my sins and throw them into the sea of forgetfulness. Cleanse me and come into my life. Holy Spirit come dwell in me right now, protect me, guide me, comfort me and lead me to all truths. I want to live a life pleasing to God to show my appreciation for Jesus' sacrifice for me. Thank you and by faith, I trust that it is already done. In Jesus Name I Pray. Amen.

www.ingramcontent.com/pod-product-compliance
Lightning Source LLC
Chambersburg PA
CBHW051200120626
46547CB00012B/1142